Penguin Books

Utterly Trivial Knowledge: Travel Trivia

Utterly Trivial Knowledge: Travel Trivia

Edited by Margaret Hickey with Lesley Venn

with special contributions by
Joseph Mirwitch and M. J. Sigurvinsson

Penguin Books

Penguin Books Ltd, Harmondsworth, Middlesex, England
Viking Penguin Inc., 40 West 23rd Street, New York, New York 10010, USA
Penguin Books Australia Ltd, Ringwood, Victoria, Australia
Penguin Books Canada Ltd, 2801 John Street, Markham, Ontario, Canada L3R 1B4
Penguin Books (NZ) Ltd, 182–190 Wairau Road, Auckland 10, New Zealand

First published by Penguin Books 1987

Filmset in Linotron Century by
Rowland Phototypesetting Ltd, Bury St Edmunds, Suffolk
Made and printed in Great Britain by
Cox & Wyman Ltd, Reading

Introduction

You have seen it in the supermarket. A parent reaches up to the shelf for a packet of biscuits and the two-year-old, sensing its big moment, is away, making its bid for freedom. It is surprising how far those bandy little legs will carry the tiny traveller; and that early proof of an inborn impulse to go places is confirmed over and over again. We run away from home with our teddies; we have competitions as to who is the first to see the sea; then we graduate to full-blown voyages. Some are content with Torremolinos, others ski down the north face of the Eiger. It's all a matter of scale.

Why do we do it? In a word – discovery. It is an old saw that travel broadens the mind, and it is also true that sitting at a desk all day broadens something else. We should, however, draw a distinction between going abroad in a homogenized cocoon and travelling. Martin Amis has pointed out that the gulf between holidaying and travelling is a wide one, and gets wider every day, so to distinguish the pure traveller who, like the pilgrim, suffers *en route* to his goal – the philosophical may see that very suffering as the goal itself – from the light-hearted tripper whose thirst for novelty and adventure is more easily quenched, we have split our quiz into six categories, as follows.

Traveller's Tales – from a real-life triple-barrelled explorer to the larger-than-real-life Baron von Munchausen who was pursued by wolves, we test your knowledge of travellers and explorers, of people and places in fiction.

On the Map – we range from pole to pole, alighting on the longests, deepests or widests of the earth, and challenge you to pinpoint the exact spot where the world splits in two. We may as well warn you we allow very little latitude on this one.

These Islands – most of us will have every sympathy with the Rochdale woman once overheard in Spain saying, 'It's very nice to go abroad, but, eeh, I do love me 'ome.' This section concentrates on Great Britain, Ireland and the lesser islands dotted around these coasts.

The Seven Seas – actually only four Cs – culture, customs, cuisine and civilization, but in these days of cuts ... It's not just the scenery that makes elsewhere different. Take the business of *siesta* – Nöel Coward reliably informs us that in Hong Kong they strike a gong and no further work is done. Let others do as the Romans do, mad dogs and Englishmen think they know better.

The Pleasure Principle – Nancy Mitford's Uncle Matthew thought that abroad was bloody and all foreigners were fiends, but some of us actually like going to see the sites and the sights, and this looks into why we go where we do. Who would trek through dense jungle in Guatemala if it were not to see the ancient ruins of Tikal? And where would Wigan be without its pier?

Last, down to practicalities. *Traveller's Travail* looks at people at work, at the nuts and bolts of transport, and throws a spotlight on the snares and pitfalls an unwary traveller may fall into. Don't book that fortnight's holiday in Burma – you can only get a visa for a week!

When you have taken this Cook's tour of the earth, you may be left like a beached whale, unable to move from the spot, but that will wear off. The greatest reward of travelling must be to stumble across something like this sign, seen in a golf clubhouse in Jinja, Uganda: 'Any Ball Falling in the Footprint of a Hippopotamus May be Moved.'

1

1. Who made which return journey carrying an umbrella going and a piece of paper coming back?
2. What is the name of the country formerly called Upper Volta?
3. In which city did Viscount Fitzwilliam found a museum?
4. Which is the only Western embassy in Ulan Bator, capital of Mongolia?
5. Which countries do you cross if you walk the Tour of Mount Blanc?
6. Which film idol died while driving his brand-new Porsche?

76

1. What globe-trotting record does Karol Wojtyla hold?
2. Which kingdom is seldom referred to by its full name of — Darussalam?
3. Where was the liner *Queen Elizabeth II* built?
4. The four bronze horses in St Mark's Square in Venice were looted from which city?
5. Where is the restaurant which numbers every duck it sells?
6. Which great bird flies tens of thousands of miles without touching land, but never north of the thirtieth parallel?

151

1. What was the subject of an early documentary film with a verse commentary by a famous English poet?
2. Where is Corregidor, nicknamed 'The Rock' during the Second World War?
3. The Paston Letters give insight into fifteenth-century English life in which county?
4. Who, or what, are the victims of the annual *mattanza* – slaughter – off the west coast of Sicily?
5. Name the racetrack near Paris where le smart set go to see the Arc.
6. Which British luxury liner was sunk by a German U-boat in May 1915?

1

1. Neville Chamberlain, who went from London to Munich and back, to speak to Hitler.
2. Burkina Faso.
3. Cambridge, in 1816.
4. The British Embassy, at 30 Peace Street.
5. France, Italy and Switzerland.
6. James Dean.

76

1. Better known as John Paul II, he is the most travelled Pope ever.
2. Brunei.
3. Clydebank, Strathclyde.
4. Constantinople.
5. In Paris. The restaurant is *La Tour d'Argent*.
6. The wandering albatross.

151

1. The night-mail train from London to Glasgow. The verse commentary was written by W. H. Auden.
2. In the Philippines, near Manila.
3. Norfolk.
4. Tuna fish, returning from the Atlantic to breed in the warmer waters of the Mediterranean.
5. Longchamp. (The *Prix de l'Arc de Triomphe* is France's top horse race.)
6. The *Lusitania*.

Q

2

1. In the winter of 1940 Franz von Werra dived through the window of a Canadian train. What was his ultimate destination?
2. Why might Gene Kelly sing his heart out on Mount Wai'ale'ale?
3. Which Buckinghamshire town has been the sometime home of Enid Blyton, Edmund Burke, G. K. Chesterton and Robert Frost?
4. Where does the selection of dishes known as the *rijsttafel* come from?
5. How do you go on a 'silent safari'?
6. '*No pasarán*' was the Spanish anti-Fascist's rallying cry. They shall not pass to where?

77

1. From which planet did the infant Superman travel to Earth?
2. The Madaba Mosaic is a map set into the floor of a sixth-century church in Jerusalem. A map of what?
3. What quality rating system, sponsored by the English Tourist Board, is available to hotels and guest-houses from 1987?
4. Which language, spoken by over 55 million people, is not known to be related to any other?
5. Now they are denied the White City, who might hare over to Harold's Cross?
6. Before British Airways it was BOAC; what was it before BOAC?

152

1. Whom did Orpheus go seeking in the underworld?
2. In an ideal world, how many nautical miles would a crow fly from North to South Pole?
3. What comes in many varieties at Alum Bay in the Isle of Wight?
4. In which country are lap dogs called 'sleeve dogs'?
5. Where might you find a friendly *felucca* heading out of town?
6. On a timetable operating the 24-hour clock, one train arrives at midnight and one departs. How are their times displayed?

2

1. Germany. He was the only German prisoner of war to escape and find his way back home.
2. Because he would be singing in the rain up to 350 days in the year – more than anywhere else.
3. Beaconsfield.
4. Indonesia.
5. By balloon.
6. Madrid.

77

1. Krypton
2. The Holy Land.
3. One to four crowns. They got the idea from Scotland where they use thistles.
4. Korean.
5. Lovers of greyhound racing. Harold's Cross is in Dublin.
6. Imperial Airways.

152

1. Eurydice.
2. 10,800 – 180 (degrees) times 60 (minutes). If the earth were a perfect sphere a nautical mile would be the distance subtended on its surface by one minute of arc.
3. The sandstone cliffs, which range from chocolate brown to strawberry pink.
4. China. They were so named because of the Mandarins' habit of carrying them in their wide sleeves.
5. On the Nile – they are traditional sailing vessels.
6. The arrival is at 24:00 hours, the departure at 00:00 hours.

3

1. Who pipped Scott to the South Pole?
2. Which planet was discovered this century, after mathematicians had predicted its existence?
3. Which famous author worked at Warren's Blacking Factory on the site of London's Charing Cross Station?
4. What, roughly, is the minimum number of reindeer a Lapp must own in order to make a living from them?
5. Near which modern capital city are the remains of Carthage to be seen?
6. Where does the A-train go to?

78

1. How did the much-travelled Victorian naturalist, Marianne North, record her finds?
2. Which city may be entered by the Damascus Gate, the Dung Gate, Herod's Gate and the Zion Gate?
3. Who, in the North-East, make a day in July a gala occasion?
4. What are the two main national dailies in the USSR?
5. Why might *Glühwein* give you that 'piste' feeling?
6. Which ships were known in the nineteenth century as 'spouters'?

153

1. Name the country discovered by a saint in 1516 and by no one else since.
2. Which capital city was known until 1924 as Kristiana?
3. What naturally divides the Men of Kent from the Kentish Men?
4. If a man were smoking an Indian *lunkah*, what would he be smoking?
5. Where will you find Cinecittà?
6. In which decade did de Havilland's Comet first appear over Johannesburg?

3

1. Roald Amundsen.
2. Pluto. They found it even though the hypothetical calculations were faulty.
3. Charles Dickens.
4. Between one and two hundred.
5. Tunis, capital of Tunisia.
6. According to the song, Harlem.

78

1. She painted flowers.
2. The old city of Jerusalem.
3. The Durham miners and fellow miners of the North-East.
4. *Pravda* and *Izvestia*.
5. Because it is a popular Austrian après-ski reviver.
6. Whaling ships.

153

1. *Utopia*, a mythical land invented by St Thomas More. The name means 'no place'.
2. Oslo.
3. The River Medway. The Men of Kent live on the east of the river, the Kentish Men on the west.
4. A strong cheroot, according to Sherlock Holmes, 'much favoured in Madras'.
5. In Rome – it is the name of the film studios.
6. The 1950s – 1952 to be exact. It was the world's first commercial jet airliner, flying the London to Johannesburg route for BOAC.

4

1. Which travel writer, when she is not *Among the Cities*, goes home to Wales?
2. What is the capital of Nicaragua?
3. Where in Suffolk could you find the scene depicted in Constable's *The Hay Wain*?
4. Chopped fish, onion, carrot, herbs and matzoh meal are the ingredients of which Jewish dish?
5. The Kröller-Müller Museum in Holland has a large collection of work by which Dutch artist?
6. What do Rubens, Molière, and Catalan-Talgo have in common?

79

1. Garrison Keillor chronicled the goings-on of which small US town?
2. What splits the world in two over the Victoria to Dover line?
3. Which town is the seat of the National Library and the University College of Wales?
4. Which island produces most of the world's crop of carob?
5. Under what name does the English cricket team travel abroad?
6. How much should you tip a porter in Lusaka, Zambia?

154

1. Shakespeare's *The Winter's Tale* refers to 'Bohemia, a desert country near the sea'. Where is Bohemia?
2. Which city in the USSR lies on approximately the same latitude as Rome, Istanbul and Chicago?
3. Where are Brechou, Jethou, Lihou and Herm?
4. Name the aboriginal musical instrument made from a hollowed-out tree-trunk.
5. Which town, noted for its mosaics, was the chief residence of the Roman Emperors from AD 404 to 476?
6. In 1972 the floating Seawise University was burnt in Hong Kong harbour. How did it begin life?

4

1. Jan Morris.
2. Managua.
3. Flatford Mill.
4. Gefilte fish.
5. Van Gogh. There is also a Van Gogh museum in Amsterdam.
6. They are among the thirty-nine names used for Trans-Europe Expresses on the railways.

79

1. Lake Wobegon, which somehow appears on no maps.
2. The Greenwich Meridian. Victoria Station is west, Greenwich is east.
3. Aberystwyth.
4. Crete.
5. England. Formerly, they were the MCC.
6. Nothing – tipping has been abolished.

154

1. In Czechoslovakia, and it is not very near the sea.
2. Tashkent.
3. They are some of the lesser-known Channel Islands.
4. The didgeridoo.
5. Ravenna.
6. As the liner the *Queen Elizabeth*.

5

1. Where might you find a clay and wattle cabin, nine bean-rows and a hive for a honey-bee?
2. What distinction can the island of Bouvet, in the South Atlantic, claim?
3. On which Scottish island is St Magnus' Cathedral?
4. Goethe, Schiller, Nietzsche, Liszt, Bach and Richard Strauss all lived and worked in which East German city?
5. Which wine, thought to be the best in Italy, comes from Montalcino in Tuscany?
6. If you arrived in Leningrad Station, where would you be?

80

1. Which Briton stopped a train, then flew to Brazil?
2. Tanganyika and Zanzibar amalgamated to form what?
3. What is Kent doing in Cumbria?
4. Baron Rothschild met with little interest when he tried to set up a wine-making industry in which country?
5. In which country are the chances both to buy a gun and to be killed by one the highest in the world?
6. In which city can you visit the Spanish Riding School?

155

1. Into which bay did Sir Francis Drake sail 'to singe the King of Spain's beard'?
2. Between which two Swedish cities does the Göta Canal run?
3. Who wrote the novel after which the Devon holiday resort, Westward Ho, was named?
4. Where is the Great Mosque, which contains the Ka'aba, or Black Stone, 'given by Gabriel to Abraham'?
5. Which cathedral did Monet paint again and again?
6. How was the first fare-paying railway powered?

5

1. On the Lake Isle of Innisfree, according to Yeats.
2. It is the most isolated in the world, being 1,500 miles from the nearest mainland.
3. Orkney.
4. Leipzig.
5. Brunello.
6. In Moscow. (The station takes the name of the destination.)

80

1. Ronald Biggs.
2. The United Republic of Tanzania.
3. The River Kent is Cumbria's fastest-flowing river.
4. Israel. The Israelis are not great imbibers, but there are attempts to revive the vineyards.
5. In the USA.
6. In Vienna.

155

1. The Bay of Cadiz.
2. Göteborg (Gothenburg) to Stockholm.
3. Charles Kingsley.
4. In Mecca, Saudi Arabia.
5. Rouen.
6. By sail – in 1807 on the Swansea and Mumbles Railway.

6

1. Which three travellers, like Webster's dictionary, were Morocco bound?
2. Where is Midway Island?
3. In what way does the Borders town of Galashiels remember the slaughter in 1337 of English soldiers, caught off guard while picking some wild plums?
4. Why might a Portuguese *fado* bring a tear to your eye?
5. Which British writer was named after a lake in Staffordshire, where his parents fell in love?
6. What name is given to the bald racing tyres on which Grand Prix cars travel?

81

1. What did Joseph Conrad call 'a dismal but profitable ditch'?
2. On to what geometric form did Mercator project the earth?
3. In the days of the Canterbury pilgrimages, which two cathedral towns were linked by the old Pilgrims' Way?
4. What gives Spanish Rioja wines their distinctive taste?
5. From where was Nosey's picture pinched?
6. What ceremony was accorded to the first Russian railway locomotive?

156

1. Virgil had a tower built on which he balanced an egg, claiming that 'when the egg stirreth so should the town of — quake.' Which town?
2. Name the capital of Morocco.
3. Which is the county of *Rebecca* and *Jamaica Inn*?
4. What is an Imperial Russian *koulibiaka*?
5. Why did the British take to the Kashmiri waters in the days of the Raj?
6. What was there to get steamed up about when the *Savannah* crossed the Atlantic in 1819?

6

1. Bob Hope, Bing Crosby and Dorothy Lamour in *On the Road to Morocco*.
2. Midway between San Francisco and Japan in the Pacific Ocean.
3. Its motto is 'Sour Plums'.
4. The *fado*, or folksongs of Portugal, are invariably melancholy.
5. Rudyard Kipling.
6. Slicks.

81

1. The Suez Canal.
2. A cylinder.
3. Winchester and Canterbury.
4. The oak casks in which the wines are matured.
5. The National Gallery. (Goya's portrait of the Duke of Wellington.)
6. At its first steaming it was put through a baptism according to the rites of the Russian Orthodox church.

156

1. Naples. (He was buried at nearby Pausillipo.)
2. Rabat.
3. Both novels by Daphne Du Maurier are set in Cornwall.
4. A salmon pie.
5. Because they were barred from buying land they settled for houseboats.
6. It was the first steam-driven vessel to do so. (It had paddle wheels.)

7

1. In 1912, Scott wrote, 'Great God! this is an awful place.' Where?
2. The Galapagos Islands are a province of which country?
3. Which is East Anglia's only west-facing holiday resort?
4. Name the strong colourless Greek drink made from grape-stems and flavoured with aniseed.
5. Where are the tallest living things in America, which John Steinbeck calls 'ambassadors from another time'?
6. Changing between two 'Intercity' trains on the German State Railways, how far should you expect to walk?

82

1. Which three travellers had 'a cold coming' of it?
2. The capital of which country, founded as a home for freed American slaves, is named after an American president?
3. Off which Norfolk resort must sailors avoid getting stuck in 'The Devil's Throat'?
4. What do Nîmes, in France, and Calicut, in India, have in common?
5. Which annual event commemorates the Emancipation Run of 1896?
6. Which Afrikaaner gave his name to a South African airport?

157

1. In 1943, Heinrich Harrar escaped from an internment camp to a country then closed to all foreigners. Which country?
2. How long is the piece of string that is as long as a cable?
3. What did the Romans build in AD 143 as a frontier from the Clyde to the Forth?
4. What would you get if you asked for 'white steak' in Israel?
5. Name the autumn festival celebrated in Bavaria in which brass bands accompany great guzzlings of wine, beer and food?
6. New York is served by three major airports. Name them.

7

1. The South Pole.
2. Ecuador.
3. Hunstanton.
4. Ouzo.
5. In the coastal mountains of Northern California. They are the giant redwood trees.
6. Across the platform. The computerized reservation system puts you in the same carriage on each train on your journey, while all Intercity trains use one platform at a station.

82

1. The Magi, in *The Journey of the Magi* by T. S. Eliot.
2. Liberia. It is Monrovia, after James Monroe.
3. The sandbanks known as 'The Devil's Throat' are off Cromer.
4. They both gave their names to a type of fabric – denim (*de Nîmes*) and calico.
5. The RAC Veteran Car Run from Hyde Park to Brighton. The emancipation in question was the raising of the speed limit to 14 m.p.h.
6. Either Jan Smuts or Louis Botha.

157

1. Tibet – he spent seven years there. The internment camp was at Dehra-Dun.
2. One tenth of a nautical mile, approximately 200 yards.
3. The Antonine Wall, Scotland's major Roman work.
4. Pork, which is widely sold in restaurants.
5. The Oktoberfest.
6. John F. Kennedy, La Guardia and Newark, New Jersey.

8

1. Where did Moses receive the Ten Commandments?
2. Which country refuses to recognize Formosa/Taiwan?
3. What puzzles visitors on the common in Saffron Walden?
4. On what day do Americans celebrate their Independence?
5. Where does the Australian Rules football Grand Final take place every year?
6. Why would an Indian feel at home driving a car in Japan?

83

1. On which islands did the mutineers from *The Bounty* take refuge?
2. Name the three Baltic republics independent between the two world wars.
3. Which two towns were added to the original Cinque Ports?
4. A large star top left with an arc of four smaller stars to its right on a red ground. Which country's flag is this?
5. What would you be eating if, in France, you thought, 'How nice and what a lotte'?
6. Where did Alcock and Brown set out from on their non-stop transatlantic flight in 1919?

158

1. On which train does the climax of Ian Fleming's *From Russia with Love* occur?
2. *Krakatoa, East of Java.* What is odd about the film title?
3. Name the giant radio telescope base in Cheshire.
4. Which city has at its heart the Grand Palace, containing the Emerald Buddha?
5. Pleasure trips between which two cities take place on the villa-lined Brenta Canal?
6. By what name is the route known which Napoleon took over the Alpes Maritimes, on his way from Elba to Paris?

8

1. On Mount Sinai.
2. China.
3. An earth maze.
4. The Fourth of July.
5. Melbourne.
6. They drive on the left in both countries.

83

1. The Pitcairn Islands.
2. Latvia, Lithuania and Estonia.
3. Rye and Winchelsea.
4. China's.
5. *Lotte de mer* is monkfish.
6. St John's, Newfoundland.

158

1. The Orient Express.
2. Krakatoa is west of Java.
3. Jodrell Bank.
4. Bangkok.
5. Venice and Padua.
6. The *Route Napoléon*.

9

1. Where did the poet muse that time might stand still at ten to three?
2. Which part of Africa was given its name by Vasco da Gama in 1497?
3. Which town in Kent holds a Dickens festival in June?
4. From which region of Spain do the dances *pasodoble* and *sevillana* come?
5. In the 1900 Baedeker for America three sights were awarded two stars – the Niagara Falls, the Grand Canyon and —?
6. Which trading company, nicknamed 'John Company', was founded in 1600 and received its charter from Queen Elizabeth I?

84

1. Stephens did the words, Catherwood did the illustrations. Where did they travel?
2. Where are the Bitter Lakes?
3. What nickname is given to the clocktower on Birmingham Council House?
4. Jansson's Temptation is a dish from which country?
5. Where, traditionally, is the first cricket match of an Australian tour of England held?
6. What is a jaunting car?

159

1. Naming her elder sister Parthenope, Greek for Naples, her parents continued their Grand Tour and named her for another city. Who?
2. What region of France did Eleanor bring to Henry?
3. What is the collective name for the islands of Inishmore, Inishmaan and Inisheer?
4. To whom are Maoris referring when they speak of 'pakeha'?
5. For those given visas, which city of the sixth-century BC attracts visitors to south-western Iran?
6. Which two countries share the longest unfortified border?

9

1. Grantchester. The poet was Rupert Brooke.
2. Natal, from the Latin *natalis*, birthday. It was discovered on Christmas Day.
3. Broadstairs.
4. Andalusia.
5. The Magnolia Gardens in South Carolina.
6. The East India Company.

84

1. Mexico. *Incidents of Travel in Yucatan* is the account of the expedition in 1841.
2. In Egypt. They are natural lakes which form part of the Suez Canal.
3. Big Brum.
4. Sweden.
5. At Arundel Castle, against Lavinia, Duchess of Norfolk's XI.
6. It is the name used in Ireland for a horse and trap.

159

1. Florence Nightingale.
2. Aquitaine, dowry for her marriage to Henry II.
3. The Aran islands, off the west coast of Ireland.
4. Any non-Maori.
5. Persepolis.
6. The USA and Canada.

10

1. Tim Severin attempted to repeat the transatlantic journey of which saint?
2. On what are errors often knocked into a 'cocked hat'?
3. Who offered his royal all to no avail on Bosworth Field in Leicestershire?
4. Imam Bayildi ('the Imam fainted') is a popular Turkish dish. What caused his swoon?
5. Where would you go to visit the Munch Museum?
6. Name the basic unit of currency in Sierra Leone.

85

1. Where did Charley's aunt come from?
2. According to tradition, Noah's Ark came to rest on Mount Ararat. Where is it?
3. Which London landmark was once lost in the Bay of Biscay?
4. Why might you expect *tapas* with your *sangria*?
5. In steering a boat through a canal bridge, why should you normally not aim for the centre of the bridge arch?
6. How do you get the operator on an American telephone?

160

1. Which country did Joseph Conrad have in mind when he wrote *Heart of Darkness*?
2. At 12 noon GMT what is the standard time in New York?
3. Where would you go to find Britain's only public astronomical observatory?
4. The shrine of Jasna Góra in Czestochowa in Poland contains a medieval and miraculous image. What does it portray?
5. What London landmark celebrates eighty years of afternoon teas in 1987?
6. Name the caravan trail which led from China across the Gobi Desert.

10

1. Saint Brendan. He wrote it up as *The Brendan Voyage*.
2. A navigational chart. The 'cocked hat' is a triangle formed by the non-intersection of 3 lines through a single point.
3. Richard III, who offered his kingdom for a horse, a horse, according to Shakespeare rather than historians.
4. Stuffed aubergines.
5. Oslo, Norway. Edvard Munch is the country's most famous painter.
6. The Leone.

85

1. Brazil – where the nuts come from.
2. In Armenia, one of the Soviet Republics.
3. Cleopatra's Needle, an obelisk on London's Embankment.
4. Because they are small delicacies eaten with the fingers to accompany drinks in Spain.
5. Because of the tow-path, the centre of the arch is not over the centre of the channel.
6. Dial 'O'.

160

1. Zaire, formerly the Belgian Congo.
2. 7 a.m.
3. Dundee, Scotland.
4. The Black Madonna.
5. The Ritz.
6. The Silk Road.

Q

11

1. Which traveller and writer cabled from Venice to his editor, 'Streets full of water. Please advise.'?
2. Between which two land masses does the Strait of Malacca lie?
3. 'Rome was built on seven hills.' Local legend says Dufftown in the Grampians was built on seven what?
4. In which country are the wine-producing areas of Hunter River Valley, Swan Valley and Barossa Valley?
5. Where in London can you see an artist's Arab abode?
6. What guides have the word 'Pneu' on their covers?

86

1. Which African lake did John Speke reach in 1858?
2. Which part of the USSR is closest to the USA?
3. In which Irish valley is there a prehistoric graveyard of kings?
4. In which country were 15,000 Dunkin' Donut bags seized, because they were printed in English only?
5. Where would you go to drink Pilsener beer at its source?
6. How often on a tour of duty does a nuclear-powered submarine need to surface for refuelling?

161

1. 'They order, said I, this matter better in France.' Whose *Sentimental Journey* began thus?
2. Why would the Israeli town of Yafo, just outside Tel Aviv, give you the pip?
3. In which London building is a wall from the old Newgate Prison incorporated?
4. Which country has the highest number of steam trains in the world?
5. Which town hosts more festivals than any other in Britain?
6. Which British car won Le Mans three years in succession?

11

1. Robert Benchley, who along with Dorothy Parker was one of the Algonquin set.
2. The Malay peninsula and Sumatra.
3. Stills. It is an important centre for the malt-whisky industry.
4. Australia.
5. At Leighton House. Lord Leighton had it built like an Arab palace. It is now the Leighton Museum.
6. The Michelin guides. *Pneu* is French for tyre.

86

1. Lake Victoria, which he named Victoria Nyanza.
2. Kamchatka.
3. The Valley of the Boyne, between Drogheda and Slane.
4. In Canada, officially bilingual.
5. Czechoslovakia. 'Pilsener' beer takes its name from the town of Plzen (in German, Pilsen), where it is still brewed on a large scale.
6. Never.

161

1. Mr Yorick, alias Laurence Sterne.
2. Because it is better known as Jaffa.
3. The Criminal Courts of Justice – the Old Bailey.
4. China.
5. Cheltenham.
6. The Bentley, before the last war.

12

1. About which country did the American writer Lincoln Steffens say, 'I have been over into the future and it works'?
2. Name one of the three main islands which make up Japan.
3. In which country is the parliament known as the Tynwald?
4. Which city in South Carolina gave the world a dance craze in the 1920s?
5. Where can you find the bones of Keats and the ashes of Shelley?
6. What do the letters v.l.c.c. signify in merchant shipping terms?

87

1. George Mikes wrote, 'There are many non-intellectual countries; — is one of the few anti-intellectual ones.' Fill in the blank.
2. Which great river runs through China, Burma, Laos, Thailand, Kampuchea and Vietnam?
3. Which city is watched over by a pair of Liver birds?
4. Where would you go to get *dim sum*?
5. Where would you go to walk the Milford Track, from Milford Sound to Lake Te Anan?
6. What colours are New York taxi cabs?

162

1. Who publicized her *Fear of Flying*?
2. Name four of the Seven Hills of Rome.
3. What name do the French give to the English Channel?
4. Where do you get a *lei* to show that you are welcome?
5. What is the predominant smell at Rotorua in New Zealand?
6. With which city does Fort Worth, Texas, share its airport?

12

1. Post-revolutionary Russia.
2. Kyushu, Honshu and Hokkaido.
3. In the Isle of Man.
4. Charleston.
5. The Protestant Cemetery in Rome.
6. Very large crude carrier, 'super-tankers' over 100,000 tons.

87

1. Australia.
2. The Mekong.
3. Liverpool.
4. A Chinese restaurant – they are steamed dumplings.
5. The South Island of New Zealand.
6. Yellow and black.

162

1. Erica Jong.
2. The Capitoline, Quirinal, Viminal, Esquiline, Palatine, Aventine and Caelian.
3. *La Manche.*
4. Hawaii.
5. Bad eggs. Rotorua is an area of hot sulphur springs.
6. Dallas.

13

1. Who has inscribed on his tombstone, 'I'd rather be here than in Philadelphia'?
2. What are the Roaring Forties?
3. Where in West London could you still get 'in for a penny' in 1980, but for half a pound in 1987?
4. Which monastic brew comes from Fécamp in Normandy?
5. Whittlesey in Cambridgeshire has a pub called 'The Letter B'. It once had three companions. What were they called?
6. To which Japanese port do boats transport passengers travelling via the Trans-Siberian Express?

88

1. Which, according to Jan Morris, is 'the ultimate money city. Its only raison d'être is gold'?
2. Which is the largest city in Scandinavia?
3. Why would it be worthwhile to take a gander at Nottingham during October?
4. Which ancient Basque capital was immortalized in the most famous painting to come out of the Spanish Civil War?
5. Where can you see Stirling work at Stuttgart?
6. The Trans-Siberian railway runs for 6,000 miles between which two cities?

163

1. Name all four places mentioned in the titles of Shakespeare's plays.
2. By what name was Volgograd formerly known?
3. Which industry has produced the 'Cornish Alps'?
4. Zimbabwe is a Shona word. What does it mean?
5. Which Indian city was coloured pink for Prince Albert's visit in 1875?
6. What name links the Douglas DC3 with an American state?

13

1. W. C. Fields.
2. The belt of strong west to north-west winds blowing all the year round in latitude 30° to 40° south.
3. The Royal Botanic Gardens at Kew. 1d. until 1951 when it became 3d., falling with decimalization to 1p in 1971. It is now 50p.
4. Bénédictine – first made in 1610.
5. The letters A, C and D.
6. Yokohama.

88

1. Johannesburg.
2. Copenhagen. (A quarter of the population of Denmark lives there.)
3. Because it holds its annual Goose Fair then.
4. *Guernica*, in the painting by Picasso.
5. At the city's new modern art gallery, designed by James Stirling.
6. Moscow and Vladivostok.

163

1. Verona (Two Gentlemen of), Venice (Merchant of), Windsor (Merry Wives of) and Athens (Timon of).
2. Stalingrad.
3. The china clay industry. The mountains are those of white spoil resulting from quarrying.
4. Venerated house, the dwelling of a chief.
5. Jaipur. Even today the houses along the main roads are pink-washed annually.
6. Dakota.

14

1. What feat was accomplished by Ferdinand Magellan's ship, the *Victoria*, between 1519 and 1522?
2. In which state is Mount McKinley, the highest mountain in the USA?
3. What is the most conspicuous object in the Vale of Avalon?
4. Which country's cuisine serves chicken in a chocolate sauce?
5. Pisa has only one leaning tower. Which Italian city has a pair which lean in opposite directions?
6. In which French *département* is the French space centre?

89

1. Where did Christopher Columbus first set foot on land in the New World?
2. Which is Europe's northernmost capital?
3. Ex-Emperor Napoleon III of France settled here in exile between 1871 and 1874. Where?
4. Mariachi and marimba music are native to which country?
5. If a Russian had a *dacha*, what would he or she do with it?
6. Which was the last country in Europe to take up railway development?

164

1. Which group left Plymouth on 6 September 1620 to escape religious intolerance?
2. The Darling and the Murrumbidgee are tributaries of which great Australian river?
3. Which is the oldest college you can visit at Cambridge?
4. Everyone knows what chopsticks are, but what are Chinese 'chops'?
5. When would it be no disgrace to be beaten by a Finn?
6. Who benefits from the *tarif sagesse* on Canadian railways?

14

1. It completed the first round-the-world voyage – without Magellan, who had been killed en route.
2. Alaska.
3. Glastonbury Tor.
4. Mexican – but it is savoury, not sweet.
5. Bologna.
6. Guyane (French Guiana) at Kourou.

89

1. On San Salvador, an island in the Bahamas, in 1492.
2. Reykjavik.
3. Chislehurst.
4. Mexico.
5. Live in it. It is a house in the country used as a summer retreat.
6. Greece.

164

1. The Pilgrim Fathers.
2. The Murray.
3. Peterhouse, or St Peter's College, founded in 1284.
4. Stone, ivory or bronze seals, used instead of a signature.
5. After a sauna. Some, but not all, Finns lightly beat themselves or their companions with birch twigs.
6. Senior citizens.

15

1. Where is the Hellespont, which Byron swam?
2. Where is Mocha, once a great coffee port?
3. The water from which spa is taken on voyages by the Royal Family?
4. Where is the largest Welsh-speaking community outside the British Isles?
5. In which city is there a hotel so large that it would take nearly nine years to spend a night in each room?
6. Where did Ferdinand and Imelda go in February 1986?

90

1. Which British novelist is buried on Mt Vaea in Western Samoa?
2. Where is the Ocean of Storms?
3. Who became Bamburgh's darling in 1838?
4. Which African country had a poet as its first head of state?
5. Why would you go all over France following a man in a yellow jersey?
6. From which city's airport do you travel into the centre aboard the Maglev, a driverless vehicle?

165

1. In 1959 the USS *Skate* made history by reaching the North Pole. What was remarkable about the ship?
2. Where is the lowest place on the surface of the earth?
3. Which English cathedral had three spires until the early twentieth century and now has none?
4. What is a Frenchman's equivalent of an Italian's breakfast *cornetto*?
5. Where can you buy goods in the Friendship shops with FEC?
6. What is served unbroken with kosher meals on the American Amtrak railway system?

15

1. In the Dardanelles – between European and Asiatic Turkey. He swam from Sestos to Abydos.
2. The Yemen Arab Republic.
3. Malvern, in Hereford and Worcester.
4. Patagonia, Argentina.
5. In Moscow – the Hotel Rossiya has 3,200 rooms.
6. To Hawaii – the Marcos régime in the Philippines was over.

90

1. Robert Louis Stevenson.
2. On the moon.
3. Grace Darling, who, with her father, saved nine men from a wrecked paddle-steamer.
4. Senegal. He is Léopold Senghor.
5. Because he is the overall leader in the Tour de France, the world's greatest cycle race.
6. Birmingham. (*Mag*netic *lev*itation.)

165

1. It was a submarine, which surfaced there.
2. The Dead Sea, in Jordan and Israel.
3. Lincoln.
4. His *croissant*.
5. In China. They are shops which take Foreign Exchange Currency.
6. The rabbinical seal. Kosher utensils are also provided.

16

1. What was the name of the 'Promised Land', overflowing with milk and honey?
2. Which two countries share the longest mutual border?
3. Which British city has two cathedrals, both built in the twentieth century?
4. How can you experience Heaven and Earth in the Rhineland?
5. Where is Britain's biennial International Air Show held?
6. When El Al introduced the first non-stop transatlantic scheduled service it used the advert, 'No goose, no gander.' What were they implying?

91

1. What form of transport does the Mekon use?
2. Which city is less recognizable by its Arabic name of al-Quds?
3. With which literary family is the town of Haworth associated?
4. Legend has it that Julius Caesar is buried here, wearing gold boots and reclining in a golden coffin. Where?
5. Why might art-loving New Yorkers miss their MOMA when away from home?
6. Whose Monthly Railway Guide was published from 1841 to 1961?

166

1. Who disappeared permanently at the Rauschenberg Falls?
2. In which country does the Limpopo River reach the sea?
3. If Nessie lives in Loch Ness, where does Morag live?
4. Americans are nuts about their pecan pie. What are pecans?
5. Who whacks a *sliotar* with a *camán* for fun in Ireland?
6. What is signified by the ringing of the Lutine bell at Lloyds of London?

16

1. Canaan.
2. The USSR and China.
3. Liverpool.
4. By eating *Himmel und Erde*, a local dish, made with potatoes, apples and blood-sausage.
5. Farnborough in Hampshire.
6. Gander Airport in Newfoundland had been used until then to re-fuel aircraft.

91

1. A personal flying saucer, which he sits on.
2. Jerusalem.
3. The Brontë family.
4. Beneath Mont Saint-Michel, in France.
5. New York's Museum of Modern Art is known as MOMA.
6. Bradshaw's.

166

1. Professor Moriarty, arch-enemy of Sherlock Holmes.
2. Mozambique.
3. Loch Morar – she is a monster too.
4. They are nuts, too.
5. A hurler. The *sliotar* is a leather ball, the *camán* an ash stick.
6. The loss of a ship. The treasure ship *La Lutine* was sunk in 1779, and only its bell was recovered.

17

1. Who 'came out of the night that was forty below', and where?
2. Where are Heaviside, Gagarin, Pasteur and Curie, which have all been on the map since the 1960s?
3. Which castle, overlooking the River Avon, has towers named Caesar, Bear and Clarence?
4. Which Spanish dish most resembles an Iranian *kuku*?
5. What serves champagne and cruises at the speed of a bullet?
6. Why might a star-crossed lover put on a white képi?

92

1. Which quintessentially English cartoonist peopled his *Classical Landscape with Figures*?
2. The Karakoram Highway, sometimes called the Eighth Wonder of the World, connects China's Sinkiang province with — ?
3. The Royal Military Canal was built as a defence against whom?
4. What is a New Zealand kumara?
5. The City Varieties Music Hall is one of the last remaining music halls in Britain. Where is it?
6. The inaugural flight of which plane in 1969 was preceded by airport authorities checking the strength of their runways?

167

1. Which US President led an expedition to Brazil at the age of 55?
2. Near which city is the mountain of Tibidabo, with its shrine of Our Lady of Montserrat?
3. William the Conqueror began it, his son, William Rufus, completed it and it still stands in London. What?
4. Which European wine-producing country drinks three quarters of its entire production?
5. Where is the Minoan capital which Sir Arthur Evans began excavating in 1900?
6. To which country was Elvis drafted as a GI?

17

1. Dangerous Dan McGrew, in the Klondike.
2. On the far side of the moon – they were photographed by the Lunar Orbiter Missions.
3. Warwick Castle.
4. A Spanish *tortilla*, an omelette containing vegetables, eaten hot or cold.
5. Concorde. To be precise, at the muzzle velocity of a .303 rifle bullet.
6. It is traditional for despairing lovers to join the French Foreign Legion – a képi is the cap worn by Legionnaires.

92

1. Osbert Lancaster – the book was about Greece.
2. Rawalpindi/Islamabad, in Pakistan.
3. Napoleon.
4. A native sweet potato.
5. Leeds, West Yorkshire.
6. The Boeing 747 jumbo.

167

1. Theodore Roosevelt.
2. Barcelona.
3. The White Tower, in the Tower of London.
4. Portugal.
5. Knossos, Crete.
6. West Germany.

18

1. Of which country did the Dutchman, Willem Janszoon, become the first authenticated discoverer in 1606?
2. What happened to Ceylon in May 1972?
3. Where can you see the Book of Kells?
4. In which country is a traditional inn called a *ryokan*?
5. On which island did a Roman Emperor and a Lancashire singer retire?
6. How did Laika make history in November 1957?

93

1. After the Portuguese navigator, Magellan, was killed here, the King of Spain conquered these islands. Which?
2. Of which country is Lusaka the capital?
3. Which English city was known to the Romans as Durovernum?
4. What is the principal ingredient of *humitas*, the Indian dish from Argentina?
5. Where would you go to sit on 'The Hill' at Sydney?
6. What was New York's John F. Kennedy Airport formerly called?

168

1. With which Greek island is the poet Sappho associated?
2. Which smart suburb of Washington DC has given its name to an American comic actor?
3. Who are the Five Sisters of Kintail?
4. What name do we give to a Mexican Indian with European (usually Spanish) blood?
5. At which New York hotel did the witty Round Table set, including Dorothy Parker, regularly meet?
6. What form of transport is known by the letters m.v.?

18

1. Australia.
2. It became Sri Lanka.
3. Trinity College Library, Dublin.
4. Japan.
5. Capri. (Tiberius and Gracie Fields, in that order.)
6. Laika, a dog, was the first living creature to orbit Earth, carried in Sputnik 2.

93

1. The Philippines. (Named Filipinas after the son of the King.)
2. Zambia.
3. Canterbury.
4. Sweetcorn.
5. Sydney Cricket Ground.
6. Idlewild.

168

1. Lesbos.
2. Chevy Chase.
3. Five mountain peaks in Ross and Cromarty.
4. A mestizo.
5. The Algonquin.
6. A ship – m.v. stands for merchant vessel.

19

1. Which traveller wrote about *A Journey Around the Coast of Great Britain*?
2. If grandfather was born in St Petersburg and father was born in Petrograd, where ought the son to have been born?
3. In which city did Peeping Tom spy on Lady Godiva?
4. Which dance, immortalized by Cole Porter, comes from the French Antilles?
5. Where is 'the world's most famous night-spot'?
6. Why is *soroche* sometimes a problem in the Andes?

94

1. Who was the explorer after whom America is named?
2. Where are the Islets of Langerhans?
3. Name the hill in County Meath which was the ancient crowning place of the Celtic Kings of Ireland.
4. Which country banned rock-and-roll in 1958 because it was thought it might injure the hips?
5. Travelling west on Route 66, where do your kicks come to an end?
6. Both Lady Chatterley and Hercule Poirot are known to have travelled on which train?

169

1. Why did Karen Blixen and her husband go out to Kenya?
2. Neptun, Jupiter, Venus and Saturn are all towns on the shore of which sea?
3. Which island is associated with St Wilfred, St Aidan and St Cuthbert?
4. What are *candomble* and *macumba*?
5. Where would you go to see where Galileo conducted his experiments with the pendulum?
6. The first word uttered on the moon was the name of an American city. Which?

19

1. Paul Theroux.
2. In Leningrad. They are all names given at different periods to the same city.
3. Coventry.
4. The beguine.
5. In Hammersmith – the Palais. (It says so over the door.)
6. *Soroche*, or altitude sickness, is commonly experienced by those unaccustomed to living at such heights.

94

1. Amerigo Vespucci, a Florentine cartographer.
2. In the pancreas – they secrete hormones.
3. The hill of Tara, near Ceanannas Mor.
4. Iran.
5. Los Angeles. (It begins in Chicago.)
6. The Orient Express.

169

1. To work a coffee plantation.
2. The Black Sea. They are in Romania.
3. Lindisfarne.
4. African-derived religions of Brazil – the former local to Salvador, the latter to Rio.
5. The Leaning Tower of Pisa.
6. 'Houston. Eagle has landed.'

20

1. What, according to J. B. Priestley, had 'annihilated the old distinction between rich and poor travellers'?
2. Which island, famous for its monoliths, is the most isolated inhabited island in the Pacific?
3. Where in Britain is the Royal Highland Gathering held?
4. Who or what gets a roasting at a North African *méchoui*?
5. What takes place in Sienna on 2 July every year?
6. To which city does the 'International Express' from Butterworth run?

95

1. How did Lenin travel to Russia on the eve of the Revolution?
2. What country was known to the Romans as Lusitania?
3. For which craft is the town of Honiton famous?
4. What meat is used in the German dish *sauerbraten*?
5. Who has priority in the sea where a pair of black-and-white flags fly above the surface?
6. What did the 1930 Road Traffic Act do to British speed limits?

170

1. 'I thought it the foulest city on earth until I saw Peking', sighed Isabella Bird, soulfully. Where?
2. The Cape of Trafalgar, scene of Nelson's famous victory, is a few miles south of which Spanish port?
3. What do the church of Walton-on-the-Naze and the churches of Dunwich have in common?
4. Which national gallery houses the Velazquez painting *Las Meninas*?
5. Which town on the Dee is known for its International Musical Eisteddfod?
6. Why were a sheep, a cockerel and a duck high-fliers in September 1783?

20

1. The bus.
2. Easter Island.
3. Braemar, Grampian.
4. A lamb, which is barbecued.
5. The *Palio*, a wild horse race.
6. Bangkok. Butterworth is in Malaysia, opposite Penang Island.

95

1. In a sealed train, passing through Germany, arriving at the Finland Station.
2. Portugal.
3. Lace-making.
4. It is hot, spiced beef.
5. Surfboarders.
6. It abolished them altogether. Results were so disastrous that a new act had to be passed in 1934 imposing the 30 m.p.h. urban limit.

170

1. Seoul.
2. Cadiz.
3. They have all been drowned by the sea.
4. The Prado in Madrid.
5. Llangollen.
6. They were the first balloonists – launched by Joseph and Etienne Montgolfier for eight minutes.

21

1. Aboard which vessel did Charlie Allnut and Rose go to Lake Tanganyika?
2. Which two cities lie submerged in the Dead Sea?
3. Which town is at the end of the Road to the Isles?
4. What do the punters bet with in Ireland?
5. How many meals a day did Cunard offer to first-class passengers on their Atlantic liners in the 1890s?
6. Which city is served by Marco Polo Airport?

96

1. Which world-travelling wordsmith, addicted to alliteration, used to invite us to his world?
2. The Liebnitz Range, reaching heights of 25,000 feet (8,000 metres), is the highest range where?
3. What have the following in common: Carlisle, Ripon, Great Yarmouth, Thurles and Ayr?
4. By what name do we know the national soup of the Ukraine?
5. Where was the most far-out place Caruso ever sang in?
6. How old must an article be to qualify as antique for the purposes of US Customs?

171

1. What unusual arrangement did Ulysses and Turner, the painter, organize for themselves on board ship?
2. Name the capital of Qatar.
3. The twisted, leaning tower of the parish church provides the most notable landmark in which Derbyshire town?
4. Which French town is noted for its lace, its cream, its castle and its racetrack?
5. What is the upper age limit for a member of the Youth Hostel Association?
6. In the late nineteenth century, what were known as 'coffin ships'?

A

21

1. The *African Queen*.
2. Sodom and Gomorrah.
3. Mallaig. The Road to the Isles is the A830.
4. The *punt* – the Irish pound.
5. Ten, including eight between 11 a.m. and 9 p.m.
6. Venice.

96

1. Alan Whicker.
2. On the Moon.
3. They are all the homes of racetracks.
4. *Bortsch*. (The soup is made from root vegetables, and *borshch* is an old Slav word for beet.)
5. In the opera house built in the depths of the Amazon jungle which inspired the film *Fitzcarraldo*.
6. 100 years or more.

171

1. They both had themselves lashed to the mast, the former to resist the siren's songs, the latter to paint a storm at sea.
2. Doha.
3. Chesterfield.
4. Chantilly.
5. There is no maximum age.
6. Vessels carrying mass emigrants to the New World, large numbers of whom died on board.

22

1. King Boris of Bulgaria was a regular on the Orient Express. How did he travel once the train crossed the Bulgarian border?
2. Where is the River Demerara, after which the sugar is named?
3. In which county is Leeds Castle?
4. Which Greek city is known to tradition as Agamemnon's capital?
5. What will you find waddling in the lobby of the Peabody Hotel in Memphis, Tennessee?
6. What fires Japan's 'bullet' trains?

97

1. Arthur Grimble, an administrator in the Gilbert and Ellice Islands, wrote a classic book of traveller's tales. Name it.
2. What is the world's highest navigable lake?
3. Which Dorset town is Europe's principal centre for the manufacture of fishing nets?
4. In which country is official and technical matter composed in *katharevousa*, while novels and poetry are composed in *dimotiki*?
5. Why do travellers, both sick and well, flock every year to the home town of Bernadette Soubirous?
6. What are you driving on if you're on top of 'washboarding'?

172

1. Which country did Rupert Brooke dub 'El Cuspidorado'?
2. Which is the world's largest stretch of continuous sandy desert?
3. 'Offa's Dyke', an Anglo-Saxon defence work, can be found where?
4. What is the predominant flavouring of a Hungarian goulash?
5. Why might a trip to Saratoga Springs, in New York State, set you up or set you back?
6. What name was given to the squadrons which located and marked targets for RAF bomber raids from 1942 on?

22

1. He took over as driver, defying anyone to stop him. He was a devotee of speed, but lacked a grasp of what signals meant.
2. Guyana.
3. Kent.
4. Mycenae. It is known to archaeologists as the centre of the great Helladic civilization.
5. A flock of ducks.
6. Electricity – every axle on the train is motored.

97

1. *A Pattern of Islands.*
2. Lake Titicaca, in the Andes.
3. Bridport.
4. In Greece.
5. Because Lourdes, where she saw the Virgin Mary in 1858, is a place of pilgrimage, and many have been, they claim, miraculously cured there.
6. Densely packed 'waves' of mud or sand, common on unpaved roads in the tropics. You need to keep up momentum to avoid being shaken to pieces.

172

1. North America, from the natives' habit of chewing tobacco and spitting.
2. Rub' al Khali, the Empty Quarter of Arabia.
3. Running close to the border between England and Wales, from Prestatyn to near Chepstow.
4. Paprika.
5. Because it is both a spa and the site of a famous racetrack.
6. Pathfinders.

23

1. Which Irishman wrote, 'I reckon no man is thoroughly miserable until he be condemned to live in Ireland'?
2. What links Cuernavaca, Mexico, with Naples?
3. Whose is the Latin epitaph in St Paul's, 'If you would see his monument, look around.'?
4. What is the official language of Surinam?
5. Where is the longest marked trail in the world?
6. Who introduced the walk-on, transatlantic Skytrain in 1978?

98

1. Who tried to claim his inheritance at Upton Country Park but was proved to be a butcher from Wagga Wagga, New South Wales?
2. How many republics are there in the USSR?
3. It used to be Nye's and now it is Neil's. Name it.
4. What can you expect if you accept an offer of 'plastic' on the Caribbean island of Montserrat?
5. Which Sicilian resort was discovered by the smart set, who began to winter there at the turn of the century?
6. Described by Herodotus over 2,000 years ago, *cufas* are still in use on the rivers Tigris and Euphrates. What are they?

173

1. Which group of travellers set out from the Tabard Inn?
2. Which island group is also known as the Friendly Islands?
3. What is dragged through the streets and destroyed by fire in the annual Shetland ceremony of Up Helly Aa?
4. OK, Maccabee and Gold Star are local beers in which country?
5. Between which states in the US does the old 'Spanish Trail' run?
6. In aviation, what do the letters SST signify?

23

1. Jonathan Swift.
2. Both cities lie under a volcano. (Popocatepetl and Vesuvius.)
3. Sir Christopher Wren. (It was written by his son.)
4. Dutch.
5. The Appalachian Trail from Maine to Georgia, more than 2,000 miles.
6. Sir Freddie Laker.

98

1. Roger Tichborne – the 'Tichborne Claimant'.
2. Fifteen.
3. Ebbw Vale, the constituency which returned Nye Bevan and Neil Kinnock to Parliament.
4. A drink of the fiery raw local rum.
5. Taormina – habitués included D. H. Lawrence and Katharine Mansfield.
6. Skin-covered, wooden-framed small boats.

173

1. The pilgrims in Chaucer's *Canterbury Tales*.
2. Tonga.
3. A replica Viking longship.
4. Israel.
5. Florida (St Augustine) and California (the Spanish missions).
6. Supersonic air transport.

24

1. What was Livingstone's last driving ambition on the African continent?
2. In which country is the bridge over the River Kwai?
3. What is often called 'a walk along the backbone of England'?
4. Why should Popeye be grateful to Iran?
5. What will Trigano sell you for a handful of holiday beads?
6. What is 'green' on Japanese 'bullet' trains, and 'soft' on a Chinese train?

99

1. In which Japanese city is *Madam Butterfly* set?
2. 'From here to Timbuctoo.' Where is Timbuktu?
3. Where in Britain do the International Paraplegic Games take place?
4. What sort of soap should be used when in a Japanese bath?
5. Which widely spoken language was first acknowledged in print dans les pages de Punch en 1978?
6. What is the name given to the traditional Arab sailing boat?

174

1. Which New Zealand bee-keeper shared the headlines with Queen Elizabeth II on 29 May 1953?
2. Which US state was created out of territory taken from Idaho?
3. Which English village was the object of close observation by the parson and naturalist, Gilbert White?
4. Where is there a local wine called Omar Khayyam?
5. How often does the village of Oberammergau put on its Passion Play?
6. Where would you find the train known as the Indian-Pacific and why is it so called?

24

1. To find the source of the Nile.
2. Burma.
3. The Pennine Way.
4. Because spinach originated there.
5. Anything for sale in the Club Méditerranée centres he set up. Beads are used instead of money.
6. The name given to first class.

99

1. Nagasaki.
2. In Mali.
3. At Stoke Mandeville.
4. None. Soaping and washing are done outside the bath, which is for sitting in.
5. Franglais.
6. A dhow.

174

1. Sir Edmund Hillary. He and the Sherpa, Tenzing Norgay, reached the top of Everest on that day.
2. Montana.
3. Selbourne, Hampshire.
4. In Egypt.
5. Every ten years.
6. It runs coast to coast in Australia – from the Pacific to the Indian Ocean.

25

1. After filming *On the Beach* there, which city did Ava Gardner find 'a good place to make a film about the end of the world in'?
2. In Lafreri's maps, which Titan was shown holding up the world?
3. Which English county is known for its annual well-dressing celebrations?
4. In Greece, they are *orektika*, in Italy *antipasto*. What are they in France?
5. Name the Islamic holy place built in Jerusalem in AD 638.
6. For a navigator, how can one 'southerly' point in the opposite direction to another?

100

1. Who were the captain and crew of the *Gipsy Moth IV* when she circumnavigated the world?
2. By what name is the Indonesian island of Kalimantan better known?
3. The oldest passenger airport in the world, opened during World War I, still has grass on the runways. Where is it?
4. Which is the Established Church of Scandinavia?
5. What did George Eastman invent in the 1890s which revolutionized travel photography?
6. Who took part in the Long March in 1948–1949?

175

1. To what depths did Captain Nemo sink?
2. Which city was Hesperides to the Greeks, and Berenice to the Ptolemites and Romans, acquiring its present name from the Arabs?
3. Where can you see the fastest duck in the world?
4. Which was the most important of the spices which drew explorers and merchants to the Spice Islands of Indonesia?
5. Why might queues in Swedish *systembolaget* be disorderly?
6. Where, in 1986, did religious leaders meet to pray for peace?

25

1. Melbourne, Australia.
2. Atlas – thus the word came to be applied to a collection of maps.
3. Derbyshire.
4. *Hors d'oeuvres*.
5. The Dome of the Rock.
6. A 'southerly' wind comes from the south, while a 'southerly' tidal stream moves towards the south.

100

1. Sir Francis Chichester, who sailed her single-handed.
2. Borneo.
3. Shoreham, in Kent.
4. The Lutheran Church.
5. Kodak's box camera.
6. The Chinese Communist Army under Mao Zedong.

175

1. *20,000 Leagues under the Sea*.
2. Benghazi.
3. At the National Railway Museum in York. The steam locomotive, *Mallard*, holds the world record – 126 m.p.h. – for a steam engine.
4. Black pepper, *piper nigrum*.
5. Because *systembolaget* are the state-run liquor stores.
6. In Assisi, Italy.

26

1. Where did Genghis Khan's grandson build his pleasure dome?
2. What are going up in the world if they are 'making', but not if they are 'taking off'?
3. On which Scottish island do climbers tackle the Inaccessible Pinnacle and the Crack of Doom?
4. Which Italian city is noted for its ham and cheese?
5. Every September, near the Polish-Russian border, millions are paid for products of 'Polish barns'. What are they?
6. Who are compelled to be backseat drivers in Yugoslavia?

101

1. Which German scientist and explorer made a study of the cold current off Peru, which is often called after him?
2. In what country is Basle's airport situated?
3. Where in Cornwall do you find the Giant's Castle and those of Cromwell and Charles in close proximity?
4. Name three of the four main regions in Chinese cooking.
5. Where are the world's highest public lavatories?
6. How would you call the police in Saudi Arabia?

176

1. On the evening of 4 October 1883, a group of frock-coated gentlemen with revolvers in their pockets assembled at the Gare de l'Est in Paris. Who were they?
2. Greenland was so called by its Icelandic colonist, Eric the Red. Why?
3. Where in England would you find Singin' Hinnies?
4. Where can you see the ancient Greek sculpture, *The Laocoon*?
5. What did Japanese Airlines re-introduce on Boeing 747s, in the early 1980s, that had been absent for thirty years?
6. What principle did foreign correspondent James Cameron recommend when it comes to taking money and clothing abroad?

26

1. Xanadu.
2. Tides. 'Making' tides are higher than each successive high tide, and vice versa for 'taking off' tides.
3. Skye.
4. Parma – Parma ham and parmesan cheese.
5. Thoroughbred Arabian horses, first introduced in the eighteenth century. Polish barns are stables where herds mingle freely.
6. Children under twelve and drunks!

101

1. Friedrich Humboldt.
2. France, at St Louis. It is connected to Switzerland by a tariff-free motorway.
3. On the Scilly Isles.
4. Cantonese, Peking, Shanghainese and Szechuan.
5. On the Matterhorn, in the Swiss alps, at a height of 12,000 ft.
6. Dial 999. (998 for Fire and 997 for Ambulance.)

176

1. Passengers on the inaugural journey of the Orient Express to Istanbul. (They feared brigands in the Balkans.)
2. To lure more colonists – it certainly sounds better than New Iceland.
3. Newcastle.
4. In the Vatican, in Rome.
5. Cubicles with (Japanese) full-size beds.
6. Work out how much you think will need of both, then double your money and halve your clothes.

Q

27

1. Hemingway's *For Whom the Bell Tolls* was based on events in which Spanish town?
2. By what vacant name is the South Eastern Arabian Desert, in Oman, better known?
3. Which town profits from being the birthplace of Robert Burns?
4. What fruit forms the base of the Mexican dip *guacamole*?
5. Who feels safe in New York's Jamaica Bay?
6. What was originally known as a Denver boot?

102

1. About which Victorian traveller did Rudyard Kipling say, 'Being human, she must have been afraid of something, but one never found out what it was'?
2. Which country is spread over 7,000 islands?
3. What are citizens of Manchester called?
4. Uxmal and Chichen Itza in Mexico are remnants of which culture?
5. Which town in Massachusetts was the scene of witchcraft trials in 1692?
6. Ruggles Brice founded a 'college' whose graduates do not take a diploma. What and where is it?

177

1. Where did R. D. Blackmore set his romantic novel *Lorna Doone*?
2. What is the capital of Corsica?
3. In which Edinburgh building was Rizzio murdered?
4. In which country do pine, plum and bamboo symbolize friendship even in adversity?
5. Where did the Engels and Marx families regularly take their summer holidays together?
6. Which Japanese mode of transport has a name meaning man, power, vehicle?

27

1. Ronda, in southern Spain.
2. The Empty Quarter.
3. Alloway.
4. Avocado.
5. Local wildlife – it is a designated sanctuary.
6. The wheel clamp, first used in Denver, Colorado.

102

1. Mary Kingsley.
2. The Philippines.
3. Mancunians.
4. The Mayan.
5. Salem.
6. Borstal in Lincolnshire – the first of the Borstals, which criminal slang has as 'colleges'.

177

1. Badgworthy Valley, Exmoor.
2. Ajaccio.
3. Holyrood Palace.
4. China. (They are known as the 'Three Friends of Winter'.)
5. At Eastbourne.
6. The jinricksha, or rickshaw.

Q

28

1. In 1923 Arthur Ferguson 'sold' part of London to a trusting American visitor for £6,000. Which part?
2. Papua New Guinea occupies one half of a geographical island. Name the other half.
3. Where in Merseyside does the sun never set?
4. Which American state is famous for its jambalaya, crawfish pie and filé gumbo?
5. Which race course has been the home of the St Leger Stakes since 1776?
6. What was the first man-made satellite into orbit?

103

1. Name the ship in which Jason set sail in search of the Golden Fleece.
2. Where in France can you find Utah and Omaha?
3. Where are the ashes of English cricket interred?
4. What is unusual about the residents of Sun City, Arizona?
5. Which of the nineteenth-century British hill stations in India earned the nickname 'Snooty'?
6. In what unusual way do all express trains enter Belgrade's main railway station?

178

1. Which explorer said, 'They can't take it away from me, can they? You never heard of a country's name being changed . . .'?
2. On the bank of which river does Lisbon stand?
3. What are caught in the traditional 'haaf' nets on the Solway estuary?
4. What is the name of the Australian Aboriginal throwing-stick, which can hurl a spear 100 metres or more?
5. Why might a Sicilian tell you to go to Bagheria?
6. What are 'shinkansen' on Japan's railways?

28

1. Trafalgar Square.
2. Irian Jaya, or Western New Guinea.
3. At Port Sunlight, built as a model village for Unilever employees.
4. Louisiana.
5. Doncaster, South Yorkshire.
6. Sputnik 1.

103

1. The *Argo*.
2. The beaches of Normandy. They were names given to American D-Day landing areas.
3. In the Long Room at Lord's.
4. Only people fifty years old or older may buy a house there.
5. Snooty Ooty – Ootacamund in Tamil Nadu.
6. Backwards.

178

1. Cecil Rhodes. Rhodesia became Zimbabwe in 1980.
2. The Tagus.
3. Salmon. 'Haaf' is from a Norse word meaning sea.
4. The woomera.
5. To see the seventeenth- and eighteenth-century baroque palaces. Bagheria was the summer retreat of the Palermitan nobility.
6. The 'bullet trains'.

29

1. Who was executed for a Voyage to Guiana – his written Apology being published two hundred years too late?
2. Where are the foodies' choice, the Chocolate Mountains?
3. Both Wat Tyler in 1381 and Jack Cade in 1450 were leaders here of rebellious assemblies. Where?
4. A young man of which nomadic people would say to his beloved, 'You have penetrated my liver'?
5. In which country can you buy an astrakhan in Astrakhan?
6. Why should airline passengers not carry fountain pens?

104

1. Which traveller wrote, 'The Trans-Siberian is *the* big train ride. All the rest are peanuts'?
2. The Great Sandy, the Great Victoria, the Simpson, the Gibson and the Sturt together make up — ?
3. What is the name given to the traditional Aran Islands boat?
4. Where is the following written over the portico? 'The earth is the Lord's and the fullness thereof.'
5. Where did Richard Wagner construct an opera house?
6. Which mode of transport is used in the annual race from Dawson to Yellowknife?

179

1. Who left his African village to settle in Celesteville?
2. How do Austrian 'corridor trains' differ from corridor trains in other countries?
3. Which Welsh town was jokingly known as 'Tinopolis' in the days when it produced 90 per cent of Britain's tin plate?
4. Prince Wencelas is the patron saint of which capital city?
5. On which two great rivers do steamers stop at Memphis?
6. Which route did prisoners take on their way to the Venetian State Inquisitors?

29

1. Sir Walter Ralegh.
2. In Southern California.
3. Blackheath, in London.
4. The Berbers.
5. The USSR.
6. Because decreasing air pressure as the aircraft climbs can cause pens to spurt ink – all over your clothes and the airline's seats.

104

1. Eric Newby in *The Big Red Train Ride*.
2. The Australian Desert.
3. A currach, a light, canvas-covered boat.
4. The old Stock Exchange building in London.
5. Bayreuth. It was completed in 1872 and was intended for the staging of Wagner's own works.
6. Dog sleds.

179

1. Babar the Elephant.
2. The corridors are portions of German and Italian territory that the trains cross, during which time no passengers are allowed to get on or off.
3. Llanelli.
4. Prague.
5. The Nile and the Mississippi.
6. They went across the Bridge of Sighs.

30

1. Who was In Patagonia in 1977?
2. Which country lies due north of the Strait of Hormuz?
3. Packwood House, Warwickshire, has a Yew Garden designed to symbolize which New Testament gathering?
4. Which nation forces down bashed neeps and champit tatties on 25 January each year?
5. This town of medicinal hot springs in Bohemia was named after the Emperor Charles IV, who discovered them. Name it.
6. What travelled from Southampton to New York in 1946 after years of war duty?

105

1. To which country did Lady Hester Stanhope exile herself, becoming one of its most influential personages?
2. Which Japanese city was the capital before Tokyo?
3. What are the colours of the Irish tricolour?
4. What is the combined worth of a nickel, a dime and two bits?
5. Name the city first settled by Cadillac in 1701 and besieged by Pontiac in 1763.
6. Which of the tunnels through the Alps was the first to be completed?

180

1. Who was the first man to have dipped a toe in the Ocean of Storms?
2. Into which sea do the mouths of the Indus open?
3. What is supposed to have extended from the Tyne to the Solway Firth?
4. Which city is known as the Protestant Rome?
5. Where did Montaigne, Mme Récamier, Wellington, Peter the Great and Disraeli, among others, go to take the waters?
6. Which Chinese vessel has a name which means 'three boards'?

30

1. Bruce Chatwyn, according to the title of his book.
2. Iran.
3. The Sermon on the Mount.
4. The Scots, in celebrating Burns Night. Haggis and whisky come into it, too.
5. Carlsbad.
6. The RMS *Queen Elizabeth*.

105

1. Syria.
2. Kyoto.
3. Green, white and orange.
4. 40 US cents. A nickel is 5c., a dime 10c. and two bits are a quarter, 25c.
5. Detroit. (The Motor City.)
6. Mont Cenis.

180

1. Neil Armstrong, the first man on the moon.
2. The Arabian Sea.
3. Hadrian's Wall.
4. Geneva.
5. To Spa, the Belgian town which gave its name to similar watering places.
6. The sampan.

31

1. Who led a small band of the good on the evil planet Mongo?
2. What is the capital of Pakistan?
3. Which town on the Tees has two large and unusual bridges?
4. If a Korean complains about a dog's 'dung dung', he doesn't mean what you think. What *does* he mean?
5. Which British city hosted its first International Festival in 1947?
6. A subsidiary of what organization originally administered the building of the German *Autobahn* system?

106

1. About which country did Voltaire write, 'It is not worth the trouble of being known. If a man would travel there, he must carry his bed'?
2. The Ruwenzori, Africa's Mountains of the Moon, run along the border between which two countries?
3. The lives of which folk are explored in the Folk and Transport Museum in Holywood?
4. The elephant's foot design is characteristic of which carpets?
5. The largest blue marlin on record was caught in 1986 off the coast of which island in the Indian Ocean?
6. In which country do the most powerful locomotives in the world operate?

181

1. Which town inspired Ewan McColl's song, *Dirty Old Town*?
2. Which is the hottest, driest and lowest place in the USA?
3. From which battle does Battle in Sussex take its name?
4. By what name is the Andalusian *cante hondo* better known?
5. Punch, Bolivar and Romeo y Julieta are all smokes from — ?
6. What can you not take on board a plane if it is 46 ins. long?

31

1. Flash Gordon, in the 1930s science fiction movies.
2. Islamabad (formerly Rawalpindi).
3. Middlesbrough. One is a transporter bridge and the other, Newport bridge, rises vertically 100 ft in under a minute to avoid obstructing shipping.
4. Its bark – 'dung dung' means 'woof woof'.
5. Edinburgh.
6. The German railways.

106

1. Spain.
2. Zaire and Uganda. They are Africa's highest range.
3. Ulster folk. Holywood, County Down.
4. Those from Bokhara, in the USSR.
5. Mauritius.
6. Switzerland, on the privately operated Berlin-Simplon line, where the electric locos put out nearly 9,000 horse power.

181

1. Salford, outside Manchester.
2. Death Valley, north of the Mojave Desert in California.
3. The Battle of Hastings, in 1066.
4. *Flamenco*.
5. Havana. They are cigars.
6. Hand luggage. 45 ins. is the maximum.

32

1. From which country did Jules Verne's *Journey to the Centre of the Earth* begin?
2. Which is the only US state named after an English county?
3. In which Northamptonshire castle was Mary, Queen of Scots, executed?
4. What is the attraction in the Indian caves at Ajanta and Ellora?
5. In which restaurant were crêpes Suzette invented in honour of one of Edward VII's popsies?
6. The rail service from Adelaide to Alice Springs is popularly nicknamed the Ghan. Why?

107

1. Which Victorian traveller wrote *Arabia Deserta*, describing his travels in Northern Arabia?
2. Which is India's westernmost state?
3. Where in Lancashire was the first Co-op opened, in Toad Lane?
4. What is the New York restaurant favoured after first nights?
5. To which country would you travel to visit the Hanging Gardens of Babylon?
6. What did Inca messengers take to help them keep on running?

182

1. Name the Portuguese navigator who made the first sea voyage from Europe to India.
2. Which two countries in Central America do not have a Pacific and an Atlantic coast?
3. Which piece of furniture hangs around in Winchester Castle?
4. Which French city is particularly associated with storks?
5. Where would you go to see America's oldest horse race?
6. How much is a Kenyan copper worth?

32

1. From Iceland – the Snaefellsnes Peninsula.
2. New Hampshire.
3. Fotheringay Castle.
4. Wall paintings, sculpture and architecture.
5. At the Café Royal, in London.
6. From 'Afghan', the nationality of the camel drivers who once provided transport in the outback.

107

1. Charles M. Doughty.
2. Gujarat.
3. Rochdale. The old shop now houses the Rochdale Pioneers Co-operative Museum.
4. Sardi's.
5. Iraq.
6. They chewed leaves from the coca plant, from which cocaine is extracted.

182

1. Vasco da Gama.
2. Belize and El Salvador.
3. The Arthurian Round Table hangs on a wall there.
4. Strasbourg.
5. Louisville, Kentucky. The race is the Kentucky Derby.
6. 10 cents – 100 cents make a Kenya shilling.

33

1. Who undertook an 'improbable voyage' across Europe, from the North Sea to the Black Sea in an ocean-going trimaran?
2. Port Moresby is the capital of which country?
3. Where in Britain do they make tarts with an almond and jam filling and a macaroon topping?
4. Name either the birthplace or the place of burial of the Prophet Muhammad.
5. What is guaranteed by a coin thrown over your shoulder into the Trevi fountain in Rome?
6. What is the unit of currency of Lebanon?

108

1. In 1503 a Portuguese sailor discovered a group of four islands in the South Atlantic. Who was he?
2. The Bridge of Friendship across the Danube joins which two socialist republics?
3. Which London church is known as 'the actors' church'?
4. What have priority over everything on wheels or legs in Amsterdam?
5. Which Bombay hotel was built to outdo the fashionable and exclusively European Watson's, which no longer survives?
6. To which shipping line does the *Princess Diana* belong?

183

1. Dead Man's Chest, in the British Virgin Islands, provided the inspiration for which novel?
2. What was Tasmania formerly known as?
3. What is the name given to the long-distance footpath between Oakham, Leicestershire, and the Humber Bridge?
4. Pelota is the national game of which European minority?
5. What is Agra's most famous tourist attraction?
6. Which aeroplane made its first flight in March 1969?

33

1. Tristan Jones.
2. Papua New Guinea.
3. At Bakewell, in Derbyshire.
4. They are Medina and Mecca, respectively.
5. Your return one day to Rome, according to the legend.
6. The Lebanese lira.

108

1. Tristan da Cunha – he gave the islands his own name.
2. Romania and Bulgaria.
3. St Paul's, Covent Garden.
4. Trams.
5. The Taj Mahal.
6. P. & O. Cruises.

183

1. *Treasure Island*, by Robert Louis Stevenson.
2. Van Diemen's Land.
3. The Viking Way.
4. The Basques.
5. The Taj Mahal.
6. Concorde.

34

1. Horace claimed, 'The Appian Way is less tiring to those who travel slowly.' Which two cities did the Appian Way link?
2. What did the Governor of the West Indies buy from the Indians for $24-worth of knick-knacks?
3. Where is Jane Austen buried?
4. What name is given to the aniseed liqueur drunk in Turkey?
5. Why do opera buffs travel to Verona in the summer season?
6. If you flew to Calcutta by mistake, what could you call yourself with some degree of appropriateness?

109

1. Robert Benchley once wrote, 'There are only two ways to travel. One is first class . . .' And the other?
2. In which country is the most northerly town in Europe?
3. Who are always standing outside their Piccadilly shop?
4. Which large tubers are a staple of a large part of Africa from the Ivory Coast to Cameroun?
5. Where could you see New Zealand's highest mountain?
6. What must be a white oval, at least 175 mm. wide and 115 mm. high, enclosing black Latin capitals at least 80 mm. high?

184

1. On his tour of the US, Oscar Wilde came across a sign in Leadville, Colorado which delighted him. What was it?
2. A map of *what* divides the world into chernozems, serozems and podzols, amongst other things?
3. What did the GLC call 'the eighth wonder of the world'?
4. Pissaladière, an onion and tomato tart, is associated with which French city?
5. Which aquatic event starts with a 21-gun salute?
6. Who worked on a Volga steamboat and as a railway guard before becoming a full-time writer?

34

1. Rome and Brindisi.
2. Manhattan.
3. In Winchester Cathedral.
4. *Raki* – it is the national drink.
5. For the open-air music festival staged in the Roman amphitheatre.
6. A Dum Dum. It is the name of the airport!

109

1. '. . . the other is with children.'
2. In Norway – Hammerfest.
3. Mr Fortnum and Mr Mason, standing on either side of the striking clock.
4. Yams.
5. In Mount Cook National Park.
6. A GB plate on a car.

184

1. 'Please do not shoot the pianist. He is doing his best.'
2. A map of soil groups. These are all Russian names which have passed into international usage.
3. The Thames Barrier.
4. Nice.
5. Cowes Week. The twenty-one brass cannons used were originally on the sailing ship, *Royal Adelaide*.
6. Maxim Gorky.

35

1. To the nearest thousand, what is the greatest number of men carried on a voyage by a single vessel?
2. Reds are normally *under* the bed, but which Ukranian river might be *in* it?
3. Where were the quayside scenes for the TV series *The Onedin Line* filmed?
4. Which 'Murphy' arrived in Ireland from Southern Chile?
5. What city includes the Lido, the Alcazar and the Crazy Horse Saloon among its well-known attractions?
6. On a boat, what does a 'lubber's line' do?

110

1. Why did Guy Gibson and company go to the Ruhr?
2. Which islands in the Aegean do you know are scattered as soon as you see their name on the map?
3. What Kentish gardens are set out in cants, sets and hills?
4. How do some fishermen in Sri Lanka keep their feet dry?
5. As of the end of 1986, which was the last British car to win Le Mans?
6. What is significant about telephone numbers beginning '800' in the USA?

185

1. Which triple-barrelled traveller recently drove his wife and a friend up the pole?
2. What is the plural of metropolis?
3. In which county is the great hill fort of Maiden Castle?
4. What is known in France as 'baby-foot'?
5. What is the chief characteristic of the megapode, a bird found only in the Andaman Islands?
6. Which disease, to which travellers were prone, caused 'scorbutic' symptoms to be exhibited?

35

1. 17,000 (16,683 to be precise), on the *Queen Mary* when used as a troopship in 1943. There were life boats or rafts for 8,000 only.
2. The River Bug.
3. At Exeter.
4. The potato, in around 1565.
5. Paris. They are all big nightclubs.
6. It is a boat's heading mark, on the bowl of a steering compass.

110

1. To bust dams.
2. The Sporades – sporadically scattered.
3. Hop gardens. Each root is called a hill, a group of hills makes a set, and a group of sets makes a cant.
4. They are stilt fishermen.
5. Aston Martin.
6. They are all toll-free over long distances.

185

1. Ranulph Twisleton-Wykeham-Fiennes. (They attempted to circle the earth from pole to pole.)
2. Metropoles.
3. Dorset.
4. Table football – all the rage in French cafés.
5. Its big feet.
6. Scurvy, caused by prolonged absence of fresh fruit and vegetables.

36

1. — Park, a Scottish surgeon, set out in 1795 to try to trace the course of the Niger. What was his first name?
2. Which river flows through Rome?
3. Which town might have lost its sparkle if Colonel Gadaffi had had his way?
4. What are the won-tons in Chinese won-ton soup?
5. Where was the first motor-racing track in the world opened?
6. What does the *dezhournaya* look after in a Russian hotel?

111

1. Which English explorer began his career as captain of a slave ship, the *Judith*?
2. By what name do we more commonly know the Wall of Ten Thousand Li?
3. Where may we see a statue erected by Lord Shaftesbury in tribute to fraternal love?
4. What is the special attraction of the Venetian lagoon island of Murano?
5. At which Kenyan hotel did HRH the Princess Elizabeth learn that she had become Queen?
6. What did Herbert Austin design for the Wolseley Sheep-Shearing Company, Birmingham, in 1895?

186

1. Who took *A Short Walk in the Hindu Kush*?
2. At 12 noon GMT what is the standard time in Tokyo?
3. Which did John Betjeman find 'the most beautiful city in these islands'?
4. Of which regional delicacy can you get a surfeit along the Gironde and Garonne rivers?
5. What is the Forbidden City of Beijing?
6. Where would you be travelling if you were on the TGV?

36

1. Mungo.
2. The Tiber.
3. Blackpool. He tried to buy the illuminations for £2 million for his tenth anniversary celebrations.
4. Small stuffed pastry parcels.
5. At Brooklands, in Surrey.
6. The *dezhournaya* is a woman who holds the keys, makes the tea and keeps an eye on the guests on her floor.

111

1. Sir Francis Drake.
2. The Great Wall of China.
3. In Piccadilly Circus – the statue of Eros.
4. The hand-blown glassware made there for the last seven centuries.
5. The Treetops Hotel.
6. The company's first three-wheeler car.

186

1. Eric Newby.
2. 21.00 hours.
3. Edinburgh.
4. Lampreys.
5. The fifteenth-century Imperial Palace complex.
6. In France, on the high-speed train (*Train à Grande Vitesse*).

37

1. Which European country became a great maritime power in the fifteenth century through the voyages of exploration sponsored by Prince Henry the Navigator?
2. By which two names was Istanbul previously known?
3. On which Hebridean island is Fingal's Cave?
4. In 1984 Australia adopted a new national anthem. What is it?
5. To which saint is the cathedral in Moscow's Red Square dedicated?
6. In 1896 the prospectors Skookum Jim and Tagish Charley put this river on the map in a big way. Name it.

112

1. In the nineteenth century many fearless travellers were members of the CMS. What was the CMS?
2. The Jungfrau, the Eiger and the Matterhorn. Which is the odd one out, and why?
3. What is an Arbroath smokie?
4. Where is the Shwe Dagon Pagoda, one of the greatest Buddhist shrines in Asia?
5. By what name is Pie Street in Kathmandu locally known?
6. In which European capital does a cast-iron elevator carry people between the upper and lower parts of the town?

187

1. Which famous author was paid to go to Mexico in the 1930s to study the effects of persecution on the Catholic Church?
2. Name all four countries which have a frontier with Greece.
3. Where is there a horse-racing museum exhibiting the pistol with which jockey Fred Archer shot himself?
4. Where do they play *A Soldier's Song* before a rugby match?
5. Where would you be if people around you spoke Magyar?
6. What type of vehicle is an Indian tonga?

37

1. Portugal.
2. Constantinople and Byzantium.
3. Staffa.
4. *Advance Australia Fair*. Formerly it was *God Save the Queen*.
5. St Basil.
6. The Klondike. They registered claims to a creek called Bonanza and sparked off the Gold Rush.

112

1. The Church Missionary Society.
2. The Matterhorn, because it stands between Switzerland and Italy. The other two peaks are wholly in Switzerland.
3. Haddock smoked whole.
4. Rangoon.
5. Freak Street. (It is full of hippies.)
6. Lisbon. The Santa Justa lift, designed by Gustave Eiffel.

187

1. Graham Greene. He described his travels in *The Lawless Roads*.
2. Albania, Bulgaria, Turkey and Yugoslavia.
3. At Newmarket, Suffolk.
4. In Ireland; it is the national anthem.
5. In Hungary.
6. A two-wheeled horse carriage, used as a taxi.

38

1. Which writer and gourmet crossed the Sahara in a wheelchair?
2. There has always been a lot of 'Carry On' up this passage, 58 kilometres long between Jamrud Fort and Torkahm. What is it?
3. What constitutes Boston's Stump in Lincolnshire?
4. If you see 'mountain chicken' on the menu on the West Indian island of Montserrat, what would you expect to be served?
5. Where were you urged to 'rise and shine' on your holidays?
6. A recent agreement reached between Spain and the UK sent shivers up and down which coast?

113

1. In what wilderness did the hero of Kurosawa's film *Dersu Uzala* lend his guiding guile to European explorers?
2. The first sailors to report back from this landmass had landed at the 'Land of Flat Stones', 'Woodland' and 'Vinland'. What is it?
3. What new kind of place was Letchworth, Herts., at its inception in 1903?
4. How many days a year are national holidays in the USA?
5. Here we find a famous temple of Apollo, a charioteer and the cave of the oracle. Where?
6. Why does the Norwegian settlement of Ekofiskbyen have good links with Teesside in England and Emden in West Germany?

188

1. Which country did Thor Heyerdahl explore before any other?
2. Which African country is completely surrounded by another?
3. By what nickname is Aberdeen sometimes known?
4. Which country has a festival calendar divided into six-day cycles, each day being 'unlucky', 'semi-lucky' or 'lucky'?
5. Where would you go to see Gaudi's fantastical architecture?
6. Why are London taxi drivers particularly wise?

38

1. Quentin Crewe went *In Search of the Sahara*.
2. The Khyber Pass.
3. The 272-ft. tower of St Botolph's church, which can be seen for miles around, is known as the Boston Stump.
4. Breadcrumbed frog.
5. At Butlin's holiday camps, before the campers revolted.
6. The so-called Costa del Crime, the east coast of Spain, where many had taken advantage of there being no extradition treaty with Britain.

113

1. The Siberian *taiga* – the explorers were Russian.
2. North America.
3. The world's first Garden City.
4. None. Each state decides its own, although most states follow the federal legal public holidays.
5. Delphi, in Greece.
6. Because it is a platform in the North Sea with oil and gas pipelines to those two areas.

188

1. Norway. He was born there.
2. Lesotho.
3. The Granite City.
4. Japan.
5. Barcelona.
6. Because they have 'the Knowledge' – slang for the test they must take.

39

1. What was the purpose of John Tradescant's extensive journeys in North Africa and Europe in the seventeenth century?
2. Name one of the two islands in the River Seine in Paris.
3. Where was Uncle Tom Cobleigh off to?
4. What gives the Greek wine *retsina* its distinctive taste?
5. The Ichen, the Test and the Kennet rivers are the big three for which sportsmen?
6. What do Auckland residents refer to as 'The Coathanger'?

114

1. Which orbiting spaceman was told to put his helmet on?
2. Streets in New York occupy approximately 35 per cent of the city's space. What is the comparable figure for Tokyo?
3. Which royal residence is known to have been Queen Victoria's favourite?
4. When the French *tricolore* is flown, which colour is next to the flagstaff?
5. What are the largest of Venice's water-buses called?
6. What were 'prairie schooners'?

189

1. Where in Africa was Rick's Bar?
2. In which country is Ushuaia, the most southerly town in the world?
3. Name the islands off the Northumberland coast which are famous for their seals and seabirds.
4. What are the Parsi Towers of Silence?
5. Where would you travel to watch the soccer club Fluminese playing at home?
6. What do airlines mean when they talk about 'dwell-time'?

39

1. He was a botanist, searching for new plants.
2. The Ile de la Cité or the Ile Saint-Louis.
3. Widecombe Fair, which is held on the second Tuesday of September in Widecombe-in-the-Moor, Devon.
4. It is flavoured with resin from pine trees.
5. Dry-fly fishermen.
6. The Auckland harbour bridge linking the city with the North Shore.

114

1. Major Tom, in David Bowie's song *Space Oddity*.
2. 10 per cent.
3. Osborne House, on the Isle of Wight.
4. Blue. (Then white, then red.)
5. *Vaporetti*.
6. The covered wagons in which the American pioneers headed Westwards.

189

1. Casablanca in the film of the same name.
2. Argentina.
3. The Farne Islands.
4. Towers where the dead are laid out to be picked clean by birds of prey, thus defiling none of the four elements.
5. Rio de Janeiro, Brazil.
6. Delays.

40

1. Which Central American country is the setting for Paul Theroux's *The Mosquito Coast*?
2. Vesuvius destroyed Pompeii, but also — ?
3. Which British waterways were formed after a thirteenth-century rise in the sea level flooded peat diggings?
4. Which birds are the protagonists of the Afghan version of cock-fighting?
5. Where is there more caviar on the move than anywhere else in the world? (Other than in fish.)
6. How is a 1 in 20 road gradient described in Europe?

115

1. Where do 'little cable cars climb halfway to the stars'?
2. Name the former Dutch possession, found on the north-east coast of South America, whose capital is Paramaribo.
3. Who took refuge in the fenland isle of Athelney, in Somerset, and there, they say, neglected his culinary duty?
4. What is a *trou normand* and what is its purpose?
5. Which game, a cross between 'Black Pool', 'Pyramids' and another game, was thought up in Madras in 1875?
6. Ships' captains are empowered to conduct which religious rites?

190

1. What Rubicon was crossed by Chuck Yeager in 1947?
2. The largest island in the world is a county of Denmark. Name it.
3. Where in Wales can you travel by the Electric Cliff Railway to look through the biggest camera obscura in the world?
4. *Gong*, *sarong* and *amok* are words from which language?
5. What made Californians flock over the state line when Las Vegas opened for business?
6. Which is the most famous crossing in the Berlin Wall?

40

1. Belize.
2. Herculaneum.
3. The Norfolk Broads.
4. Partridges. They battle until one appears the victor, not to the death.
5. On board the *QE2* – the world's largest caviar buyer.
6. 5 per cent.

115

1. San Francisco, where, in the song, Tony Bennett left his heart.
2. Surinam.
3. King Alfred, of the burning cakes.
4. In the middle of a large meal a Norman breathes deeply and swallows a glass of calvados, 'to aid digestion'.
5. Snooker. (The other game was billiards.)
6. Burials and baptisms, but not marriages.

190

1. The sound barrier. He flew an experimental aircraft at 670 m.p.h., equivalent to Mach 1.015.
2. Greenland.
3. At Aberystwyth.
4. Malay-Indonesian.
5. Gaming, which outside of racetracks was and is illegal in California.
6. Checkpoint Charlie.

41

1. *Unconditional Surrender* is a fictionalized account of Evelyn Waugh's experiences in the 1940s as a liaison officer in which country?
2. Into which sea does the Volga flow?
3. Which British island has a name which means 'the Englishman's Isle'?
4. What are felafel?
5. Where is Jeremy Bentham not buried?
6. What was the 'first' achieved by Alexei Leonev in March 1965?

116

1. Who was tied down and imprisoned by the Lilliputians on his travels?
2. Name the northerly wind that sweeps over the west coast of Africa.
3. What is the name given to the original site of Salisbury?
4. In descending order, black, red and yellow horizontal stripes comprise the flag of which country?
5. In which city is the world-famous Copacabana beach?
6. Name the Nova Scotian businessman who founded the first transatlantic steamship line in 1839.

191

1. Which Mediterranean island does Lawrence Durrell describe in his book *Prospero's Cell*?
2. What was the capital of Australia before Canberra?
3. Whose remains may be found in St Paul's Cathedral in a sarcophagus made for Wolsey and appropriated by Henry VIII?
4. Which island inspired a mixture of bourbon, red vermouth, Angostura bitters and a maraschino cherry?
5. What is Bombay duck?
6. Where would you be if you landed at Kastrup Airport?

41

1. Yugoslavia.
2. The Caspian.
3. Anglesey.
4. Fritters made from ground chick peas. It is a Middle Eastern dish.
5. He is not buried anywhere. But his embalmed body can be seen seated inside a glass case at University College, London.
6. He was the first man to walk in space.

116

1. Lemuel Gulliver.
2. The harmattan.
3. Old Sarum.
4. West Germany.
5. Rio de Janeiro, Brazil.
6. Samuel Cunard.

191

1. Corfu.
2. Melbourne.
3. Nelson.
4. Manhattan.
5. Dried fish fried and served as a side dish with Indian food.
6. In Copenhagen.

42

1. In which city does Shakespeare's *Romeo and Juliet* take place?
2. It is known to the Chinese as Qomolangmafeng, to the Nepalese as Sagarmatha and to the Tibetans at Miti gu-ti Cha-pu long-na. What is it?
3. Which three towns host the Three Choirs Festival?
4. The King of which country has as one of his titles 'The Possessor of the Four and Twenty Umbrellas'?
5. What is the main attraction of Hong Kong's Aberdeen harbour?
6. How many pins do American plugs have?

117

1. Who gave the Pacific Ocean its name?
2. Which American city has districts known as Chelsea, Cambridge and Somerville?
3. What is fishy about Dublin Bay prawns?
4. Which is the most sacred mountain in Japan?
5. The John Muir Trail through the Sierra Nevada starts at Whitney Portal, California, and ends in a valley famous for its dramatic rock scenery. Which valley?
6. What did they first get Wright in 1903?

192

1. Which popular British novelist made an *English Journey* in the autumn of 1933?
2. How many time zones are covered by the USA?
3. What is the Portland Race?
4. Where might you be offered an undistilled drink made from cactus, known as *pulque*?
5. In which European city is *Comme Chez Soi* the place to eat?
6. What do the letters ETA mean in the context of travel?

42

1. In Verona.
2. Mount Everest.
3. Gloucester, Hereford and Worcester.
4. Thailand.
5. The floating seafood restaurants.
6. Two, both flat.

117

1. Magellan.
2. Boston.
3. They are small Scandinavian lobsters which used to be sold in Dublin markets, and are perhaps better known as *scampi*.
4. Fuji-Yama, home of a goddess from whom the imperial family was believed to have descended.
5. The Yosemite Valley.
6. Powered flight – the brothers Wright.

192

1. J. B. Priestley.
2. Seven. (Four coast-to-coast, with three more in Alaska.)
3. A wild-foamed tidal rip, off Portland Bill.
4. In Mexico. (Distilled cactus drinks are mezcal and tequila.)
5. Brussels.
6. Estimated time of arrival.

43

1. Which climber and explorer abandoned Unilever for Patagonia in 1962?
2. Known as hurricanes in the Atlantic, what are tropical storms known as in the Pacific?
3. Name the Cornish town famous for its wreckers in the nineteenth century and its surfers in the twentieth.
4. Of what are *nan* and *paratha* Indian versions?
5. Name the idiosyncratic house in Virginia built by President Thomas Jefferson.
6. When did the red Rolls-Royce badge turn black?

118

1. Where did Abraham pitch his tent and Jacob have his dream?
2. Name the stretch of water separating New Zealand's North and South Islands.
3. Which town is the home of the Open University?
4. Which town in the Netherlands is renowned for its blue and white china?
5. Where, in 1979, was the last 'real' MG sports car made?
6. Who is generally credited with the invention of the 'pound' lock, the standard form of waterway lock to this day?

193

1. Where, according to Noël Coward, do they 'strike a gong, and fire off the Noon Day Gun'?
2. What name was given to the interior of eastern Africa by Greek and Roman geographers, such as Ptolemy?
3. In what county are the Bedford Levels?
4. The men of which country voted to enfranchise women in 1984?
5. In Yugoslavia, what service is performed by Jadrolina?
6. The Kremer Prize offered £50,000 to the first person to complete a figure of eight course one mile long. How?

43

1. Chris Bonnington.
2. Typhoons.
3. Bude.
4. Bread.
5. Monticello.
6. After the death of Charles Rolls, who was the first Briton to die in a flying accident.

118

1. At Bethel, a town outside Jerusalem. (Many Nonconformist chapels are named after it.)
2. Cook Strait.
3. Milton Keynes.
4. Delft.
5. At Abingdon.
6. Leonardo da Vinci.

193

1. In Hong Kong.
2. Azania.
3. Cambridgeshire.
4. Liechtenstein.
5. It is the state ferry system, linking the Adriatic islands to each other and to the mainland.
6. Flying by muscle power alone. The prize has been won.

44

1. On a pilgrimage down which river did St Ursula and her 11,000 virgins meet their doom?
2. By what name are the Sandwich Islands now known?
3. Where did Drake announce that the Armada could wait, but his bowls couldn't?
4. Which dance from Cuba became popular in the 1920s?
5. In which city is there a race course called Happy Valley?
6. There are three NASA Space Centers in the USA. Name one of them.

119

1. Genoa has produced two great explorers. Name one.
2. What is unique about the island of Chausey?
3. To which communities is the name An Ghaeltacht given?
4. Which brandy comes from the French *département* of Charente?
5. Which country is renowned for its cedar trees?
6. If you land at O'Hare Airport, in which city do you find yourself?

194

1. About which country did Rebecca West write *Black Lamb and Grey Falcon*?
2. What is the modern name of Benares, the holy city on the River Ganges?
3. Where is Anne Hathaway's cottage and who was she?
4. What ingredients make up the Tunisian drink *lait de poule*?
5. Which city does the writer V. S. Pritchett find 'the most instantly talkative in Europe'?
6. From which ship did Captain Benjamin Briggs and his crew disappear in 1872?

44

1. The Rhine, probably near Cologne, and probably only eleven virgins.
2. The Hawaiian Islands.
3. At Plymouth Hoe. (Some have it that he actually said his bowels could not.)
4. The rumba.
5. Hong Kong.
6. The Huntsville in Alabama, the LBJ in Texas and the JFK in Florida.

119

1. John Cabot and Christopher Columbus.
2. It is the only French island in the Channel Islands.
3. Those throughout Ireland where Irish is the spoken language in general use.
4. Cognac.
5. Lebanon.
6. Chicago.

194

1. Pre-war Yugoslavia.
2. Varanasi.
3. In Stratford-upon-Avon. She was Mrs William Shakespeare.
4. A whizzed-up blend of fruit, milk and egg.
5. Dublin.
6. The *Marie Celeste*.

45

1. 'And the wildest dreams of Kew are the facts of . . .' where, according to Rudyard Kipling?
2. Which great Canadian river, now named after its Scottish discoverer, was first called the River of Disappointment?
3. In which British city is there a 'People's Park'?
4. Where, according to American Indian legends, was a fountain of eternal youth to be found?
5. Where is Wittett's Gateway of India?
6. Which travellers began to be spied on towards the end of the 1970s?

120

1. Which Victorian novelist described her travels in India, in company with the Governor-General of India, in her book *Up the Country*?
2. By what name is Bait Lahm, in the Middle East, more familiar?
3. Name the island in the Firth of Forth from which the gannet takes its scientific name.
4. Give an alternative nickname for Old Glory.
5. Where is the largest Duty Free Shop in Europe?
6. The Russian rouble can be divided into 100 – what?

195

1. Which painter and poet collaborated for many years to produce the *Shell Guides* to the English and Welsh counties?
2. Name all five of the Great Lakes.
3. Which stately home was the first to include a safari park?
4. What would you do if an Indian gave you a Thums Up?
5. What would you have on your feet if you were 'schussing down the fall-line'?
6. What invention of the Chinese Hsia Dynasty should the independent traveller never be without?

A

45

1. Kathmandu.
2. The Mackenzie.
3. Glasgow.
4. On the island of Bimini, in the Bahamas.
5. Bombay. It is a stone archway built to commemorate the visit of King George and Queen Mary to India in 1911.
6. Lorry drivers, with the introduction of the tachograph, known as 'the spy in the cab'.

120

1. Emily Eden. Her brother, George, was the Governor-General.
2. Bethlehem.
3. Bass Rock. (Sula Bassana is the scientific name.)
4. The Stars and Stripes – the US national flag.
5. Schiphol Airport, near Amsterdam, Holland.
6. Kopecks.

195

1. John Piper and John Betjeman.
2. Lakes Superior, Huron, Michigan, Erie and Ontario.
3. Longleat, in Wiltshire.
4. Drink it. It is India's Coca-Cola.
5. Ski boots and skis.
6. The compass, c.2,600 BC.

46

1. Using Homer as his guide, what did Heinrich Schliemann discover in the nineteenth century?
2. Approximately how long is the coast of Africa in proportion to that of Europe?
3. From which town in Britain did Queen Victoria get the jet for her lugubrious jewellery?
4. Where, until 1896, might a man have taken several wives and executed sinners?
5. 'I "legged it" through the Dudley Tunnel'. Legged what?
6. QANTAS is Australia's overseas airline. What do the letters stand for?

121

1. Which capital city was described in a Tom Stoppard play as 'the Reykjavik of the South'?
2. Name the road which runs from British Columbia to Alaska.
3. Which is England's deepest lake?
4. What is the basic ingredient of *nasi goreng*?
5. Where can you see Christ preaching at a Thames regatta?
6. To what use did aircraft manufacturers put 6-lb frozen chickens?

196

1. Who commanded the voyage of the *Endeavour* to Tahiti in 1768 to observe the transit of Venus across the sun?
2. 600 million years old, the largest rock in the world is sometimes called Uluru. By what other name is it known?
3. Which British town became a city by Royal Charter in 1977?
4. Which Central American state abolished its army in 1948?
5. Which town boasts five 18-hole golf courses, including the Royal Birkdale?
6. What name is given to illegal immigrants who cross into the United States from south of the border?

46

1. The remains of the ancient city of Troy – present-day Truva, in Turkey.
2. One tenth. Africa is a far larger continent, but its coast is very smooth.
3. Whitby.
4. In Salt Lake City, Utah, home of the Mormons.
5. A narrow boat. 'Legging' involves pushing the boat by walking your feet against the tunnel walls. No engines may be used in the Dudley tunnel.
6. Queensland and Northern Territory Air Services.

121

1. Edinburgh, more euphemistically known as the 'Athens of the North'.
2. The romantically named Top of the World Highway, which runs 1,500 miles across North America.
3. Wast Water, in Cumbria.
4. Rice. It is Indonesian fried rice, served with a selection of spicy sauces and side dishes.
5. At Cookham, Berkshire, in Stanley Spencer's painting.
6. To test the strength of the windscreens in case of 'bird-strikes'.

196

1. Captain James Cook.
2. Ayers Rock.
3. Derby.
4. Costa Rica.
5. Southport, Merseyside.
6. 'Wetbacks'.

47

1. In which city did Dostoevsky set *Crime and Punishment*?
2. Which island is dominated by Mauna Loa and Mauna Koa?
3. What are the star attractions at the RSPB reserve at Loch Garten, Speyside?
4. Which Irish dish, made from potatoes and cabbage, was a hot favourite for fast-day festivities?
5. Where can you find Cleopatra's beach close to Pompey's Column and Cavafy's house?
6. What do Iceland, Laos and Chad have in common, concerning railway networks?

122

1. Where was Bunyan imprisoned while he wrote *A Pilgrim's Progress*?
2. São Jorge, Santa Maria and São Miguel are islands in which Atlantic archipelago?
3. Where was the first iron, as opposed to wood or stone, bridge built?
4. Why does the Hudson River in New York run green on 17 March?
5. Which city did Kenneth Tynan put on the theatrical map?
6. What was started by Nero in AD 67, finished in 1893 and reduced the trip from Piraeus to Italy by about 200 miles?

197

1. Name the 'rose-red city, half as old as time'.
2. Which country is called South West Africa by South Africa?
3. The folly called McCaig's Tower in Oban is a near-replica of which classical Roman landmark?
4. In which city is Christ's burial cloth supposedly found?
5. What is the name given to the cocktail made from gin, cherry brandy, Cointreau, red wine and lemon juice?
6. Where was the Morris Oxford two-seater car first built?

47

1. In St Petersburg (now Leningrad).
2. Hawaii – they are mountain peaks.
3. Ospreys, which returned to Britain to breed in the late 1950s after a forty-year absence.
4. Colcannon.
5. At Alexandria, Egypt.
6. They have no railways.

122

1. In Bedford.
2. The Azores.
3. Ironbridge in Staffordshire.
4. It is part of the annual St Patrick's Day celebrations.
5. *(Oh) Calcutta.*
6. The Corinth Canal.

197

1. It is Petra, according to James Elroy Flecker.
2. Namibia.
3. The Colosseum in Rome. Built in the 1890s, it provided work at a time of unemployment.
4. Turin – the Turin Shroud.
5. A Singapore gin sling.
6. At Cowley, Oxford, in 1913.

48

1. Why did Amundsen make an about-face in 1909?
2. Name the South American country once known as Upper Peru.
3. On which island do the pubs give out free rum and milk cocktails on 'Milk-a-Punch day', the first Sunday in May?
4. The Dragon King rules over the Realm of the Dragon. By which name is this country better known?
5. The Sibelius Memorial stands in which city?
6. What do the letters EVA signify to an astronaut?

123

1. Which ruined sandstone castle in Warwickshire inspired Sir Walter Scott's novel of the same name?
2. Papeete is the capital of which island in French Polynesia?
3. The largest area of fresh water in the United Kingdom is in Northern Ireland. What is it called?
4. Which country, famous for its raw fish dishes, was declared officially vegetarian in the fourteenth century?
5. Where is the tomb of Tamberlaine?
6. What is pinyin?

198

1. Which Viking founded the first settlement in Greenland?
2. What is the colloquial name given to the area of New York City south of Houston Street near Greenwich Village?
3. Who flock to Minsmere in Suffolk?
4. Children are allowed on the White House lawn on one day every year. Which?
5. Name Copenhagen's famous amusement park.
6. What significance do the letters BG and MG have in an Indian railway timetable?

48

1 He had been intending to reach the North Pole, but when
   he heard Peary had already got there, he set off for the
   South Pole instead.
2. Bolivia.
3. Alderney in the Channel Islands.
4. Bhutan.
5. Helsinki. He is Finland's greatest composer.
6. Extravehicular activity or a space walk.

123

1. Kenilworth.
2. Tahiti.
3. Lough Neagh.
4. Japan.
5. Samarkand.
6. The official transcription of Chinese characters.

198

1. Eric the Red, also called Eric Thorvaldsson.
2. SoHo. (*S*outh of *Ho*uston.)
3. Bird watchers. It is one of the most visited RSPB
   reserves.
4. On Easter Monday, for the traditional Egg Rolling
   contest.
5. The Tivoli.
6. Broad gauge and metre gauge, indicating the track width.

49

1. Grace Metalious wrote about the steamy goings-on in which US town?
2. A giant statue of Christ the Redeemer, made of bronze from old cannons, stands on the frontier of which two countries?
3. What binds the Princess of Wales to Dolgellau in Gwynedd?
4. Which country's men can expect to live the longest?
5. In what sport can you try to carry off the One Ton Cup?
6. Lord Kitchener called it 'a pretty mechanical toy', and its name was originally a ploy to confuse Germans. What?

124

1. Where did the king sit, 'supping the blude-red wine'?
2. The largest island in the Baltic, it was once a Viking settlement, and Visby is its chief town. What is it?
3. Which Yorkshire town is famous for its toffee?
4. People of which nation spend a lower percentage of their income on food yet consume more food per person than any other?
5. What is the 'iron sail' on a sailing barge?
6. How is the Queen described on a British passport?

199

1. Who is Australia's peripatetic Minister for Culture?
2. What is the maximum distance you would need to travel to catch your train on the British mainland?
3. In which Cheshire town do they shop in Rows?
4. Which country has a million and a half registered 'senior footballers'?
5. Which Antipodeans promise you ninety but only give you sixty-four?
6. Which form of transport was conceived during the American Civil war by a balloon observer with the Union Army?

49

1. Peyton Place.
2. Chile and Argentina. It commemorates the peaceful settlement of a boundary dispute in 1902.
3. Her wedding ring was made from gold mined in the district.
4. In Sweden. The average male life expectancy is 75·79 years.
5. Yachting. It refers to the weight of the boats.
6. The (water) tank.

124

1. In Dunfermline. (According to the ballad, *Sir Patrick Spens*.)
2. Gotland.
3. Harrogate.
4. The USA.
5. The engine.
6. Her Britannic Majesty.

199

1. Sir Les Patterson, by courtesy of Barry Humphries.
2. 110 miles by road. (From Southead, on the Mull of Kintyre.)
3. Chester. The Rows are medieval streets lined by balustraded walkways.
4. China.
5. New Zealanders. Ninety Mile Beach isn't.
6. The Zeppelin, which was launched in 1900.

50

1. Who took a trip to the moon, courtesy of Professor Calculus?
2. In which desert did Mark Thatcher get lost?
3. Abbotsbury in Dorset is the only place where Britain's heaviest native birds are 'farmed'. What are they?
4. What is the equivalent of the Red Cross in Islamic countries?
5. Which American fast-food favourite is associated with Nathan's Eatery on Coney Island?
6. Stansted or no Stansted, which airport advertises itself as London's third?

125

1. Who led the first party to reach the North Pole?
2. Why was Mesopotamia so named?
3. From which Devonshire port did Richard the Lionheart set sail for the Third Crusade in 1190?
4. Which country produces more feature films than any other?
5. The Ailsa course was chosen for the 1977 and 1986 British Open Golf championships. Where is it?
6. You can get 'abeam' of any ship, but to what sort of ship can you get a 'beam up'?

200

1. Which traveller, writer and soldier was killed while riding his nickel-plated Brough Superior?
2. In which country are earthquakes so mild that one which moves a chair rates eight on the local Davison's Scale?
3. Where is the London headquarters of the Royal Academy?
4. Where would you go to eat a pizza in its home city?
5. What oriental facilities were to be found at London's Jermyn Street and Russell Square, but are no more?
6. What travellers follow where their SINS lead them?

50

1. Tintin and Snowy.
2. The Sahara.
3. Mute swans. They are the only colony of managed swans in the world. In the Middle Ages they provided a staple part of the diet for the abbey which used to be there.
4. The Red Crescent.
5. The hot dog, which originated there.
6. Schiphol Airport near Amsterdam, on account of the large number of flights between there and airports throughout Britain.

125

1. Robert Edwin Peary, an American naval engineer.
2. Its name comes from the Greek, 'between rivers', namely the Euphrates and the Tigris.
3. Dartmouth.
4. India – sixteen times more than Britain.
5. Turnberry in Ayrshire. The course belongs to the Turnberry Hotel.
6. A Starship, as in Captain Kirk to *Enterprise*, 'Beam me up, Scotty.'

200

1. T. E. Lawrence (Lawrence of Arabia).
2. The UK.
3. Burlington House, Piccadilly.
4. Naples.
5. Turkish baths.
6. In a submarine. It is the Ship's Internal Navigation System.

51

1. Who was the first woman traveller to be elected Fellow of the Royal Geographical Society?
2. Easter Island is the possession of which country?
3. Where in Ireland would you go to acquire the gift of eloquence?
4. In which country is Pushto the main language?
5. If you were fixing to mosey on down Wyatt Earp Boulevard to the Boot Hill Museum, where would you be?
6. Traffic drives on the right in only one of Britain's remaining colonies. Which?

126

1. By what name was China known to the West in medieval times?
2. If it is midday in Iceland, what time is it in Ghana?
3. Which city has no Roman Catholic cathedral, even though 95 per cent of its citizens are Catholic?
4. In which American state is the region called the Bluegrass?
5. Which is Australia's biggest horse-racing event?
6. If you saw a sign in France saying '*Douanes*', where would you be?

201

1. Which British explorer entered the holy cities of Medina and Mecca, forbidden to non-Muslims, disguised as a Pathan?
2. What is the Southern Hemisphere's equivalent of the Aurora Borealis?
3. Name the castle in Kent, restored by Lord Astor, where Henry VIII courted Anne Boleyn.
4. Where does the *coco de mer*, a double coconut, come from?
5. Where do you slide down the slippery slope of the Cresta run?
6. When might a traveller be smeared with treacle and flour and drenched with water?

51

1. Isabella Bird.
2. Chile.
3. Blarney Castle, to kiss the Blarney Stone.
4. In Afghanistan.
5. In Dodge City, Kansas.
6. Gibraltar.

126

1. Cathay.
2. Midday. Both are as Greenwich Mean Time.
3. Dublin.
4. In Kentucky.
5. The Melbourne Cup.
6. At a customs post.

201

1. Sir Richard Burton.
2. The Aurora Australis.
3. Hever Castle.
4. From the Seychelles. (The island of Praslin, more
   particularly.)
5. At St Moritz, in Switzerland.
6. When first 'crossing the line' (the Equator).

52

1. What voyaging feat did Dick Rutan and Jeana Yeager achieve in December 1986?
2. Name the two capital cities on the banks of the River Plate.
3. Where is there a stone bridge across the Atlantic Ocean?
4. Tokay is a renowned wine of which country?
5. Which country has an army made up of model soldiers with feet of clay?
6. Name the Russian vehicles drawn by three horses abreast.

127

1. Where is Lake Chargoggagoggmanchauggagoggchaubunagungamaugg?
2. Saudi Arabians do not touch alcohol, but they do have ports. Name the chief one.
3. Which is the only land-locked county in Wales?
4. Which German city was known as the 'Florence of the North'?
5. In which country can you drink the local White Cap and Tusker beers?
6. What significance has a motorway sign showing the letters Khz?

202

1. Which city did Kipling call 'the city of dreadful night'?
2. By the terms of the Louisiana Purchase, Thomas Jefferson bought the Mississippi Valley for $27 million. From whom?
3. Which castle was the childhood home of Queen Elizabeth the Queen Mother and the birthplace of Princess Margaret?
4. Smetana's tone poem *The River* is the national anthem of which country?
5. Every year in Alice Springs they hold a regatta jocularly known as Henley-on-Todds. What is unusual about the yachting and sculling events?
6. What is the maximum time a tourist may spend in Burma?

52

1. They flew non-stop around the world without refuelling, in their lightweight plane, *Voyager*.
2. Montevideo, Uruguay, and Buenos Aires, Argentina.
3. Off the coast of Scotland. The Hebridean island of Seil is reached from the mainland by crossing 'the Atlantic Bridge'.
4. Hungary. It is golden, sweet and strong.
5. China. In Xian there is an army of life-size terracotta figures.
6. A troika.

127

1. In the USA – at Webster, Massachusetts. It is an Indian name meaning 'I fish on my side, you fish on your side and no one fishes in the middle.'
2. Jeddah.
3. Powys.
4. Dresden.
5. Kenya.
6. It gives the radio frequency of local traffic information.

202

1. Calcutta.
2. Napoleon.
3. Glamis Castle.
4. Israel.
5. They take place on a dry river bed. (The organizers insure against rain.)
6. Seven days.

53

1. Name the earthly paradise in James Hilton's *Lost Horizons*.
2. Which country has the highest annual mean temperature?
3. Which poet moved in 1665 from London to Chalfont St Giles to escape the plague?
4. What is the chief ingredient of the Middle Eastern dish *hummus*?
5. Where can you see Danish sculptor Edvard Eriksen's most famous work?
6. The world's first STOLport is in London's Docklands. What does STOL stand for?

128

1. Who to whom? 'Sir, a man who has not been in Italy is always conscious of an inferiority, from his not having seen what it is expected a man should see.'
2. Name the three largest islands in the Mediterranean Sea.
3. Europe's largest artificial hill is in Wiltshire. Name it.
4. Italy, France, Spain and Portugal changed from the Julian Calendar in 1582. Which European country changed in 1923?
5. Where is the Ashmolean Museum, Britain's oldest public museum?
6. Whose son, as its General Manager until 1878, took the family travel firm to a leading international position?

203

1. Two British writers had houses at Port Antonio, Jamaica. Name one.
2. What percentage of the earth's surface is covered by sea?
3. Which is England's smallest city?
4. Prokofiev composed an air celebrating this Russian form of transport. Name it.
5. What is let down at a ceilidh?
6. Where is the world's longest undersea tunnel?

53

1. Shangri-la, supposedly in Tibet.
2. Libya.
3. John Milton. (The cottage where he finished *Paradise Lost* may be visited.)
4. Chick peas, plus sesame seed paste, olive oil, lemon juice and garlic.
5. In Copenhagen. It is The Little Mermaid, sited by the harbour.
6. Short Take Off and Landing.

128

1. Dr Johnson to Boswell.
2. Sicily, Sardinia and Cyprus.
3. Silbury Hill. Archaeologists believe the earthworks were started *c.* 2,600 BC.
4. Greece.
5. Oxford.
6. Thomas Cook. The son was J. M. Cook, the firm Thomas Cook & Son.

203

1. Ian Fleming and Nöel Coward.
2. 70·8 per cent.
3. Wells, in Somerset.
4. The troika.
5. One's hair. It is an informal gathering for music and story in Ireland and Scotland.
6. In Japan, between the islands of Honshu and Hokkaido.

54

1. John Dillinger spoke very highly of Ford cars in his line of business and once wrote to Henry Ford to say so. Who was he?
2. Where on earth is Panagaea?
3. Where, in Cornwall, do Bronze Age burial mounds surround vast saucer aerials?
4. In which country are *fusilli*, *farfalle* and *fettucine* to be found, and what are they?
5. Where would you go to see the Tourist Trophy races?
6. What is the difference between a supercharger and a turbocharger in automobiles?

129

1. How were the Tolpuddle Martyrs sent round the world?
2. Why Can Dead Men Voting Twice produce the right result?
3. In which Scottish castle was Duncan murdered in *Macbeth*?
4. 30 million plastic bricks make up what, where?
5. What is Jordan's close rival to the Israeli resort of Eilat?
6. Which guide-book did Ford Prefect use on his travels?

204

1. 'The bar . . . stood on the highest point . . . ten feet above sea level. It was called . . . "The Up and Atom". It did not prevent several of us getting madly drunk.' Where and when?
2. It changed its mouth by 250 miles in 1852, only its last twenty-five miles are navigable, and it empties into the North Pacific. Which river?
3. Where does a lop-eared pig with black patches come from?
4. Why do Sri Lankans always look forward to the next full moon?
5. Where, according to the Temperance Seven, is the grass greener?
6. What was the goal for pilgrims in the Middle Ages on the route of Santiago?

54

1. A notorious 1930s gangster in the American Midwest, one of the first men to be killed by FBI agents.
2. Everywhere. It is the name of the single land mass which geologists believe existed before it split into continents.
3. At Goonhilly Downs.
4. They are all types of pasta found in Italy.
5. The Isle of Man.
6. The former drives air into the engine by fan, the latter recycles the exhaust gases.

129

1. They were transported to Botany Bay.
2. CDMVT, as a mnemonic for Compass Deviation Magnetic Variation True, describes the sequence of corrections for converting a compass bearing to a true value.
3. Cawdor Castle. Macbeth became Thane of Cawdor.
4. Legoland, in Denmark.
5. Aqaba – five miles from Eilat across the head of the Gulf of Aqaba.
6. *The Hitch-hiker's Guide to the Galaxy*, published on Ursa Minor.

204

1. Bikini Atoll in the Pacific, the night before the first peacetime atom-bomb explosion in 1946, described by James Cameron.
2. The Hwang Ho, or Yellow River, which runs through China.
3. Gloucester. It is the Gloucester Old Spot, also known as the Orchard Pig.
4. Because the day of the monthly full moon (Poya) is a public holiday.
5. Pasadena. The song of the same name was their theme tune
6. Santiago de Compostela, the cathedral town in Galicia, associated with St James. (Santiago means St James.)

55

1. From whence did Paul Theroux set out in *The Old Patagonian Express*?
2. Which Yugoslavian lake has been designated a UNESCO National Treasure?
3. Which is the last bridge across the Thames before it reaches the sea?
4. Which Greek island is noted for being the site of the first school of philosophy, and for its wines?
5. In which state can you picnic at Hanging Rock?
6. Which London Underground station has the same name as one on the Paris Métro?

130

1. Which writer spent his boyhood at Hannibal, Missouri?
2. Which country is made up of two distinct regions, separated by 400 miles of the South China Sea?
3. Where was the Prince of Wales invested in 1969?
4. What is the native habitat of an animal which feeds only on the tenderest leaves of eucalyptus?
5. Whose tooth is stuck in Kandy?
6. Where would you buy a copy of the *Penguin News*?

205

1. Henri Mouhot, a French naturalist, rediscovered the ruins of Angkor whilst on an expedition into which country's jungle?
2. Mount Kosciusko is the highest peak in which country?
3. Where is part of the South further north than any part of the North?
4. What is the official language of the Philippines?
5. Who makes it into the Mile High Club?
6. Which island did Richard the Lionheart annexe *en route* from the Third Crusade?

55

1. Boston, Massachusetts.
2. Lake Ohrid.
3. Tower Bridge.
4. Samos. (Pythagoras founded the school.)
5. South Australia.
6. Temple.

130

1. Mark Twain.
2. Malaysia. (The Malay Peninsula is cut off from the north-west coastal area of Borneo.)
3. At Caernarvon Castle.
4. Australia. It is the koala bear, which selects only one of the hundreds of varieties available.
5. Buddha's. The Tooth Relic was brought to Sri Lanka in the fourth century AD.
6. In the Falkland Islands.

205

1. Kampuchea. (Angkor was the Khmer capital for most of the period between AD 800 and 1400.)
2. In Australia, in New South Wales.
3. In Ireland. Malin Head is further north than anywhere in Northern Ireland.
4. Tagalog.
5. People who have made love during a flight.
6. Cyprus.

56

1. Which rock singer travelled Africa from Timbuktu to Addis Ababa, in 1985?
2. If a traveller told you about the King penguins he had seen inside the Arctic Circle, what conclusion would you draw?
3. Name the beauty spot in Devon where the East Dart and the West Dart meet.
4. Why might you be served pap in a Korean restaurant?
5. Where would you go to hear a Festival of Nine Lessons and Carols, held on Christmas Eve?
6. What is unusual about the time kept by clocks aboard the Trans-Siberian Express?

131

1. Who went to snap factories in Russia, Gandhi in India, and was the only woman war photographer in the Korean War?
2. What is the capital of Somalia?
3. What shape are the columns of the Giant's Causeway?
4. Carp forms the main Christmas Eve dish for many German families. Which part of the fish is saved for luck?
5. What is baked in Yorkshire and Lancashire on Guy Fawkes Night?
6. Which aid to travellers was thought up by Professor Zamenhoff a hundred years ago?

206

1. Which author of animal stories told of his travels among the Marsh Arabs of Iraq in *A Reed Shaken by the Wind*?
2. Where is the world's highest railway station?
3. What is the Green Bridge of Wales?
4. The pagoda was originally a tower over a Buddhist shrine. What do we call something similar in India and Sri Lanka?
5. Which Mediterranean swimmer risks being beaten if caught?
6. What idea for a fixed link is abhorred by Flexilink?

56

1. Bob Geldof.
2. That he was a liar. Penguins live at the South Pole.
3. Dartmeet.
4. Because *pibim pap* is the name for mixed vegetables on rice.
5. King's College Chapel, Cambridge.
6. It is always Moscow time, varying by up to seven hours from local time.

131

1. Margaret Bourke-White.
2. Mogadishu.
3. Hexagonal.
4. A scale. Each person at the meal keeps one.
5. Parkin – a spicy, treacly kind of gingerbread.
6. Esperanto.

206

1. Gavin Maxwell.
2. At Galera in Peru, on the Huancayo line. It is 15,700 ft. high.
3. A natural arch formed in carboniferous limestone in the Castlemartin Peninsula of Pembrokeshire.
4. A stupa.
5. The octopus, which it is believed needs to be beaten 100 times to make it tender enough to eat.
6. The Channel tunnel. Flexilink is the name of the consortium of ferry companies opposed to its construction.

57

1. To which island do Muslims believe that Adam and Eve fled after being cast out of Eden?
2. It is known to the Greeks as Kerkyra. And to us?
3. Where is Ireland's Poisoned Glen?
4. From which fruit is the Tunisian spirit *boukha* distilled?
5. Which dog will give you a ride all over North America?
6. What does a Turk do with his *gulet*?

132

1. The Bell Rock and its lighthouse became famous by reason of Southey's ballad. What is it called?
2. The better known Staten Island is in New York. Where is the other?
3. On which Hebridean island are there more red deer than people?
4. What is an Indian thali?
5. During the Middle Ages the seat of the papacy was for a time not in Rome but in France. In which town?
6. Who broke the speed record from Russia to Paris in 1812?

207

1. Henry Stanley's most famous words as an American were, 'Doctor Livingstone, I presume?' What nationality did he have at birth, and what at death?
2. In 1981 how many times fewer people were there per square kilometre in Australia than in Great Britain?
3. Which canal saves a long boat trip round the Mull of Kintyre?
4. Who might offer you a tinnie with your barbie?
5. Which feat of modern engineering was declared open by Jayne Mansfield?
6. From which Heathrow Terminal does Concorde operate?

57

1. Sri Lanka, formerly Ceylon.
2. As Corfu.
3. In the heart of Donegal's highest mountains. (It is named after a poisonous plant, Irish spurge, which grew there.)
4. Figs.
5. The greyhound. (Greyhound Line buses.)
6. He sails it. It's the equivalent of a caique.

132

1. *The Inchcape Rock.*
2. Off the southern tip of Argentina, a little north-east of Cape Horn.
3. Jura. The name means Deer Island.
4. A tray with a complete meal contained in little bowls called *katori*.
5. Avignon. The Palace of the Popes is still standing.
6. Napoleon. Having retreated from Moscow he left his army and went as quickly as possible to Paris.

207

1. British in both cases. Born in Wales, he was adopted by an American but re-adopted British nationality at fifty. (He also fought on both sides in the American Civil War.)
2. One hundred times fewer.
3. The Crinan Canal, which is only nine miles long.
4. An Australian. A tinnie means a can of beer, a barbie is a barbecue.
5. Chiswick Flyover, in West London.
6. Terminal 4.

58

1. Which lone yachtsman falsified the records, then could not stand the shame?
2. Which country is jointly ruled by two 'Co-Princes', the President of France and the Spanish Bishop of Urgel?
3. Its address is No. 1, London. What?
4. Which is the first state among the fifty US states?
5. Wimbledon for the British, Flushing Meadow for the Americans and — for the French. Where?
6. Which is the last major nation to link up to international direct dialling?

133

1. In which land did both Nebuchadnezzar and Bob Marley live?
2. On which Canary Island are the Fire Mountains?
3. What was Callandar, in Scotland, called when its citizens' ailments filled Dr Finlay's Casebook?
4. Which city is the home of *bouillabaisse*?
5. Name the four US Presidents who can be seen on Mount Rushmore.
6. Which morbidly named device on a train saves lives?

208

1. Where did Butch Cassidy and the Sundance Kid die?
2. The Egyptian city of Luxor was built on the site of which ancient city?
3. In which city has a Midsummer Fair been held on Midsummer Common since the Middle Ages?
4. How can a tree crop, much cultivated in the West African forest zone, be said to be the real thing?
5. Benedictine monks found the water of which Staffordshire town ideal for brewing?
6. The calamitous destruction of which bridge was chronicled by William McGonagall?

58

1. Donald Crowhurst.
2. Andorra.
3. Apsley House, London residence of the Duke of Wellington, now the Wellington Museum.
4. Delaware.
5. Stade Roland-Garros in Paris. They are all venues for the Grand Slam tennis tournaments.
6. China. It has no international code as yet.

133

1. Babylon. The former was its king and the latter a Rastafarian, who use the word to mean a place of exile.
2. Lanzarote.
3. It became familiar to viewers as Tannochbrae.
4. Marseille – it is a rich fish soup.
5. Washington, Lincoln, Jefferson and Theodore Roosevelt. Their portraits are carved out of the rock.
6. The Dead Man's Handle, which operates if the driver loses his grip on the brake lever.

208

1. In a shoot-out in San Vicente, Bolivia.
2. Thebes.
3. Cambridge.
4. It is the kola nut, from which the different brands of fizzy cola are derived.
5. Burton-on-Trent. The monastery has gone but the brewing lives on.
6. The Tay Bridge.

Q

59

1. Robert O'Hara Burke and William John Wills achieved a traveller's 'first'. Which?
2. What lies at latitude 66·5° North?
3. What connects Sir Clough Williams-Ellis with Patrick McGoohan?
4. Where does an Arab put his tarboosh?
5. Where can you go to Hell and back, without being singed?
6. In 1638, the Emperor of Japan closed the ports to all foreigners except. . . ?

134

1. Who wrote a book subtitled *On Foot to Constantinople from the Hook of Holland to the Middle Danube*?
2. Which is the largest of the American states?
3. In memory of which Dubliner was a bridge named most recently?
4. Where does Baron Samedi, a black-swathed god of the dead, roam around?
5. Where in Paris would you find the ashes of Abelard and Héloise?
6. From which country are the Gurkha regiments recruited?

209

1. Which navigator, born in Genoa and a naturalized citizen of Venice, explored the mainland of North America for the English King Henry VII?
2. Which city has the largest French-speaking population outside France?
3. In which seaside town did Débussy compose *La Mer*?
4. Name the strong red wine which comes from Eger in the north of Hungary.
5. Where would you travel to see incredible heavyweights indulging in sumo wrestling?
6. Name the theme of EXPO 86.

59

1. They made the first south–north crossing of Australia in 1860.
2. The Arctic Circle.
3. The fantasy village of Portmeirion in Wales. The former created it, and it was the setting for the TV series *The Prisoner*, in which the latter starred.
4. On his head. It is a cap like a fez.
5. In Norway, where the post office in the town of Hell does a roaring trade franking letters.
6. The Dutch.

134

1. Patrick Leigh-Fermor. The book is *A Time of Gifts*.
2. Alaska.
3. Luke Kelly, one of the group the Dubliners.
4. In Haiti. He is a voodoo god.
5. In Père la Chaise cemetery.
6. The mountain kingdom of Nepal.

209

1. John Cabot.
2. Montreal.
3. In Eastbourne.
4. Bull's Blood. The name comes from the very deep colour, rather than any additives.
5. Japan.
6. Transport. It was held in Vancouver, British Columbia.

60

1. Which Spanish conquistador discovered Florida?
2. In Scandinavia there is a zone of trees which grow for up to 200 metres above the coniferous zone. Which trees?
3. Why might Philip Larkin and Amy Johnson have been familiar with scrimshaw work?
4. Which country sends a Christmas tree for Trafalgar Square each year?
5. Name Dublin's international rugby stadium.
6. Where were the first traffic lights used in New York put?

135

1. Where in Britain was the Holy Grail reputedly brought by Joseph of Arimathea?
2. Which territory was sold in 1867 to America for $7·2 million?
3. Which forest belongs to the City of London?
4. Which country produces the widest choice of beer in the world?
5. Where did King Edward VII swap his crown for a Homburg?
6. What feat must one perform to be called *Al-Haj* or *Haji*?

210

1. Which city did Billy Graham find the most moral city he had visited?
2. The island of Hispaniola is shared by which two countries?
3. Which London bridge is closest to the finish of the Oxford and Cambridge Boat Race?
4. Which mountain range has been honoured in music by Aaron Copland?
5. Where would you be if you found yourself stuck in GUM?
6. 'Never mind the quality, feel with width.' To which European railway system is at least the second part most applicable?

60

1. Ponce de Leon.
2. Birches.
3. Because Hull, their home, has Europe's largest collection of these carved and decorated whalebones and walrus tusks.
4. Norway. A tradition started by King Haakon VII in gratitude for having been allowed to set up a wartime government in London.
5. Lansdowne Road.
6. They were mounted on to the waistcoats of policemen on point duty.

135

1. To Glastonbury.
2. Alaska, by Tsar Alexander II.
3. Epping Forest.
4. Belgium. (And they drink about 128 litres per head every year!).
5. At Baden Baden, the fashionable German spa.
6. The title indicates that the person has made a pilgrimage to Mecca.

210

1. Melbourne, Australia.
2. The Dominican Republic and Haiti.
3. Chiswick Bridge.
4. The Appalachians.
5. In Moscow – it is the city's leading store.
6. Spain's. The standard gauge is 5 ft. 6 ins., compared with the 4 ft. 8 ins. of most European systems.

61

1. Which traveller, most famous for his origins, went to the Galapagos Islands aboard the *Beagle*?
2. Where was a statue of Nelson erected in Trafalgar Square twenty-one years before its London counterpart?
3. Which river running through Cardiff evokes a nickname given to sons of Wales?
4. We are not in Calais, but here are the Burghers. Where?
5. Of the seven ancient wonders of the world, which two may still be visited?
6. How many classes of seating are there aboard Concorde?

136

1. To which lake did Tristan Jones make a journey by boat?
2. The Great Barrier Reef runs along the coast of which Australian state?
3. Where in Britain is there a famous mathematical nail-less bridge which, dismantled in the nineteenth century, could not be reassembled without nails?
4. What part of the world does pepperpot soup come from?
5. On a waterway how often should you blast off at someone to ask them, 'What the hell do you think you are doing'?
6. What is colloquially known as the 'Boeing Bug'?

211

1. Who flew through the air with the greatest of ease?
2. In what major geographical feature have the world's earliest signs of pastoral civilization been found?
3. There are two cricket clubs at Lord's. Name both.
4. Which country is the home of the *Wiener schnitzel*?
5. Name the former Palace of the Ottoman Sultans, now a museum.
6. What had to be tall enough for a gentleman wearing an opera hat to climb into without removing his hat?

61

1. Charles Darwin, who then produced *The Origin of Species*.
2. Bridgetown, Barbados.
3. The Taff. (Taffy)
4. Rodin's famous sculpture is on London's Embankment, not far from Charing Cross.
5. The Pyramids and the Tomb of Mausolus, at Halicarnassus.
6. One only.

136

1. Lake Titicaca. He journeyed from the mouth of the Amazon.
2. Queensland.
3. Cambridge.
4. The Caribbean. It's hot!
5. Five times – short ones.
6. The Boeing Corporation emblem, which looks like a fly caught on a round sticky label.

211

1. 'That Daring Young Man on the Flying Trapeze'.
2. The Great Rift Valley in East Africa.
3. Marylebone and Middlesex.
4. Austria.
5. The Topkapi Museum in Istanbul.
6. A hackney cab.

62

1. Which remarkable feat did Sir Vivian Fuchs achieve when he was fifty?
2. What is unusual about Lake Mungo in New South Wales?
3. Where would you to to see 'the noblest barn in Europe'?
4. Which people of the north of Pakistan are reputed to live to a great age on a diet of apricots and water?
5. Where in Germany is Hitler's Eagle's Nest mountain retreat?
6. If you were offered a charpoy during your travels in the East, what would you do with it?

137

1. Which Danish navigator explored the strait which separates Siberia from Alaska?
2. Where is this? 'Six suburbs in search of a city.'
3. Where would you go to view the Duke of Wellington's funeral carriage?
4. Which city transformed a disused railway station into a museum in 1986?
5. Where does the Fremantle Doctor operate?
6. What is a *samlor* in Thailand?

212

1. In whose hands did the town of Laugharne, south of Carmarthen, become Llaregyb?
2. In the Katmai National Park, Alaska, is the Valley of Ten Thousand Smokes. Why is it so named?
3. Where are the bird reserves of Skokholm Island and the island of Skomer?
4. Which area of France is renowned for its truffles?
5. The very oldest living trees in the world are the bristle cone pines. Where are most of them to be found?
6. What does a *gettone* enable you to do in Italy?

62

1. He led the first crossing of Antarctica, in 1958.
2. It has been dry for 16,000 years.
3. St Paul's church in Covent Garden, so described by its architect, Inigo Jones.
4. The Hunzas. Hunza apricots are the very champagne of apricots.
5. In Berchtesgaden, in the south-east. The house is now a restaurant.
6. Sleep on it. It is a type of string bed.

137

1. Bering, after whom it is named.
2. Los Angeles.
3. The crypt of St Paul's cathedral.
4. Paris. The Gare d'Orsay became the Musée d'Orsay, dedicated to nineteenth-century art.
5. Off the coast of Western Australia. It is a strong, persistent wind.
6. It is a three-wheeled, two-seat vehicle propelled by motor scooter, or auto-rickshaw.

212

1. Dylan Thomas in *Under Milk Wood*.
2. Because it is an area of intense volcanic activity.
3. Off the coast of Wales.
4. Périgord.
5. In California's White Mountains.
6. To make a telephone call. It is a telephone token.

63

1. From where did EB elope with RB?
2. Which Portuguese Overseas Province occupies a small island in the Canton River, China?
3. In which county is the Caldon Canal, running from Etruria to Froghall to be found?
4. Which country is the world's biggest importer of fish?
5. If you were given a Nobel Prize, where would you go to collect the award?
6. Name the two objects in the hands of the Statue of Liberty.

138

1. Where would you look for a civilization which Plato believed existed 9,600 years before his day?
2. Lapland extends over four countries. Name them.
3. Where does the Queen spend her summer holidays?
4. Kafka was born there, *Don Giovanni* was first performed there and Casanova wrote his memoirs some miles outside it. Which city?
5. Which was the world's first national park?
6. What is IATA?

213

1. Where, according to Fred Allen, is 'a place where people from Iowa mistake each other for stars'?
2. Which Himalayan state merged with India in 1975?
3. Which 'white horse' is the only prehistoric one in the country?
4. When do you run a higher than normal risk of getting your shins kicked in Chipping Campden, in Gloucestershire?
5. Where is the world's smallest cathedral?
6. Why should visitors to London feel gratitude to the designer Paul E. Garbutt?

63

1. Wimpole Street. (Elizabeth Barrett eloped with Robert Browning.)
2. Macao.
3. Staffordshire.
4. Japan.
5. Stockholm.
6. She holds a book of laws in her left hand, and a torch in her right.

138

1. Under the waves. It is the lost world of Atlantis.
2. Norway, Sweden, Finland and the USSR.
3. At Sandringham House, in Norfolk.
4. Prague.
5. Yellowstone, Wyoming, established in 1872.
6. The International Air Traffic Association – the trade association of the world's airlines.

213

1. Hollywood.
2. Sikkim.
3. The one carved in the hillside at Uffington, in Oxfordshire.
4. During the annual Dover Games, founded in the seventeenth century, which include the rural sport of shin-kicking.
5. At Murray Bridge, South Australia.
6. He designed the London Transport Underground map.

64

1. Why did globe-trotter Phileas Fogg think he had failed to win his wager, to travel round the world in eighty days?
2. To go from the north of Senegal to the south, one has to pass through which country?
3. The Mebyon Kernow are fighting for the independence of which part of Britain?
4. Who painted what eating scene on the refectory wall of the Monastery of Santa Maria delle Grazie in Milan?
5. Where would golfers go to observe the rules of golf where they were first drawn up?
6. Why were certain sea travellers to the Far East posh?

139

1. In which part of Greece is the Mani?
2. In the ancient world, it was known as Mons Calpe, one of the two Pillars of Hercules. What is it?
3. Which stadium has held Britain's largest soccer crowds?
4. Name the island country where Malay, Mandarin, Tamil and English are all official languages.
5. What building did Nathaniel Hawthorne describe as 'the center and heart of America'?
6. In 1901, which capital city could, for the first time, be reached in four days by train instead of six months by trek?

214

Who were the Rajahs Brooke?
Which great river runs through Andalusia?
Who converge on Appleby-in-Westmorland in Cumbria each June?
What causes the red-stained lips and teeth of many Indians?
In which African country did Muhammed Ali fight in a contest for the World Heavyweight Boxing championship?
If you arrive at Leonardo da Vinci Airport, where are you?

64

1. Because he had failed to allow for the International Dateline.
2. The Gambia. It is a tongue of land dividing Senegal in two.
3. Cornwall.
4. Leonardo da Vinci painted the *Last Supper*.
5. At the Royal and Ancient Golf Club, St Andrews.
6. Because they specified they wanted their cabins Port Out Starboard Home, so as to be always in the shade.

139

1. The Peloponnese.
2. Gibraltar.
3. Hampden Park, in Glasgow – over 140,000.
4. Singapore.
5. The Capitol, in Washington DC.
6. Kampala, capital of Uganda, on the completion of the East African Railway from Mombasa.

214

1. An Englishman, James Brooke, travelled East, and ended up in 1841 as Rajah of Sarawak. Two more Rajahs continued the dynasty.
2. The Guadalquivir.
3. Gipsies from all over Britain gather for Britain's largest horse fair.
4. Chewing *paan*, a mixture of spices, slaked lime and betel nut wrapped in a leaf, used as a digestive.
5. Zaire.
6. In Rome.

65

1. What unique feat did a white man, a black man and four Eskimos achieve on 6 April 1909?
2. Which country is administered jointly by the British and the French?
3. Which town in Kent did Elizabeth I establish as a naval town by ordering the building of a dockyard?
4. Where is the Adi Granth, the sacred book of Sikhism, to be found?
5. Where can you see Botticelli's *The Birth of Venus*?
6. Why did Australians give up LSD in the Sixties?

140

1. Who set out on her first journey to West Africa in 1893 and returned in 1894 to pursue 'beetles, fishes and fetish'?
2. Which country straddles eleven time zones?
3. Which World Championships takes place annually in front of the Chequered Skipper pub in Ashton, Northants?
4. What is the most common cheese found in Greece?
5. Who was the prime developer of Sardinia's Costa Smeralda?
6. In 1562 John Hawkins inaugurated a trade run between Sierra Leone and the West Indies. What was his cargo?

215

1. On which city did R. K. Narayan base his Malgudi novels?
2. What is the name of the atoll 800 miles from Tahiti, site of France's atomic testing ground?
3. Which is the fox-hunting capital of the world?
4. What fruit is used in a traditional French *clafouti*?
5. Where would you go to see what J. Paul Getty has done to Herculaneum?
6. Which capital city is largely heated by volcanic sources?

65

1. They reached the North Pole.
2. New Caledonia/Nouvelle Calédonie.
3. Chatham.
4. In the Golden Temple at Amritsar.
5. The Uffizi, Florence.
6. They changed over from the pound to the Australian dollar in 1966.

140

1. Mary Kingsley.
2. The USSR.
3. The conker championships.
4. Fetta.
5. The Aga Khan.
6. Slaves

215

1. Mysore, India.
2. Mururoa atoll.
3. Melton Mowbray – meeting place of the Cottesmore, the Belvoir and the Quorn Hunts.
4. Cherries. It is a kind of batter pudding from the Limousin.
5. To Malibou, California. The John Paul Getty Museum is a reconstruction of a villa in Herculaneum.
6. Reykjavik.

66

1. The song is well-known – *Guantanamera*, meaning 'woman of Guantanamo'. Where is it?
2. Which city has been Polish, then Austrian, then independent, Austrian again and is today Polish?
3. Where is the birthplace of Sir Winston Churchill?
4. What is a *nimbu soda*?
5. What could you first drive into in New Jersey in 1933?
6. What was unique about Nadar's balloon, which ascended with fourteen people on 4 October 1863?

141

1. Which US president commented, 'It is indeed a great wall.'?
2. What do the British call Lac Leman?
3. Which Scottish island is a place of pilgrimage and burial ground for chiefs and kings?
4. Why might a *gang pet* raise a warm flush in Thailand?
5. How can it be said that East Berliners go out on a spree?
6. What contribution did Kirkpatrick Macmillan make to the world of transport?

216

1. Which Venetian merchant spent twenty-four years exploring China and the east?
2. What is the southern boundary of the Northern Lights, or Aurora Borealis?
3. What is strictly men only on Caldy Island?
4. Ischia is Italy's biggest buyer of which unusually flavoured ice-cream?
5. Why does the Southern Aurora appear nightly between Sydney and Melbourne?
6. In which South American country can you shoot right up the Devil's Nose?

66

1. In Cuba.
2. Krakow.
3. Blenheim Palace.
4. Fresh lime juice diluted with soda water and served straight, or with sugar or salt, in India.
5. The first drive-in movie theatre.
6. It was the first to have steering apparatus.

141

1. President Nixon, on visiting the Great Wall of China.
2. Lake Geneva.
3. Iona. St Columba founded a monastery there in AD 563 and Duncan and Macbeth, among others, lie in St Oran's cemetery.
4. *Gang pet*, or 'hot curry', is a common Thai dish.
5. Because the River Spree runs just south of the city.
6. He was the blacksmith who invented, but did not patent, the bicycle.

216

1. Marco Polo.
2. The Arctic Circle.
3. Only men are allowed into the monastery of the Cistercian monks who farm the island.
4. Spaghetti.
5. It is an overnight luxury train.
6. Ecuador. It is a 5.5 per cent section of gradient on the railway line between Quito and Guayaquil.

67

1. Which poet was buried on the Greek island of Skyros in 1915?
2. There are three main groups of Pacific Islands. Name two.
3. Which British city has a network of canals more extensive than that of Venice?
4. What livestock is on sale at a Pyrenean *pottok* sale?
5. What is the name of Florida's most famous theme park?
6. What is the naked truth about the letters FKK on a German beach?

142

1. Who met whom at Ujiji, and then travelled on together to Lake Tanganyika?
2. Denmark is made up of over 500 islands. On which island does Copenhagen stand?
3. In which cathedral was Archbishop Thomas à Becket murdered?
4. Which Italian city is celebrated for the violins made there?
5. In which country is the famous fortress built by the Crusaders, the Krak des Chevaliers?
6. Where would you have gone in Massachusetts in the nineteenth century if you wanted a whale of a time?

217

1. Which Nobel Prize-winner made the first crossing of Greenland?
2. Which northern seaport is the capital of Latvia?
3. Which National Trust property in Yorkshire has a Temple of Piety and monastic ruins in view?
4. Which Asian country's politicians are on a National Diet?
5. The Faubourg Saint-Honoré, Yonge and Bloor, and the Ginza. Attach the appropriate cities to these famous streets.
6. Which luxury liner made her final voyage to Long Beach, California, where she was made into a civic centre?

67

1. Rupert Brooke.
2. Melanesia, Micronesia and Polynesia.
3. Birmingham. (Most are underground, however.)
4. Ponies. Pottoks are the native ponies of the Pyrenees.
5. Disneyworld.
6. That it is an official naturist beach.

142

1. Stanley met Livingstone.
2. Zealand.
3. Canterbury, Kent.
4. Cremona.
5. In Syria.
6. Nantucket, the greatest whaling port.

217

1. The Norwegian, Fridtjof Nansen.
2. Riga.
3. Studley Royal. The monastic ruins are Fountains Abbey.
4. Japan's. The parliament sits in the National Diet Building.
5. Paris, Toronto and Tokyo.
6. The *Queen Mary*.

68

1. Where did George Orwell fail to find the sea?
2. Grub, Snob, Red Skin and Jolly Boy are islands in which Indian archipelago?
3. Name the ancient form of boat still used by fishermen on the River Teifi at Cardigan.
4. What is the main ingredient of the Indian drink *lassi*?
5. Where is the Waterfront on which Marlon Brando worked?
6. Which bank is known locally as the Honkers and Shankers?

143

1. 'Rome, Italy, is an example of what happens when the buildings in a city last too long.' Who wrote this?
2. In which country do the headwaters of the River Nile rise?
3. Queen Elizabeth I is reported to have been on the ice daily in the winter of 1565. Where did she skate?
4. Why would you cross the river from Ahmedabad, in India, to see a spinning wheel?
5. On which Caribbean island did Captain Horatio Nelson marry local widow Frances Nisbet?
6. Why are 'Belisha beacons' so-called?

218

1. In 1889 Sir Arthur Gordon reported that inter-tribal disputes in Tonga had ceased since the introduction of which game?
2. Where would an old idolator feel at home in Burma?
3. In which national park are the Hardknott and Wrynose passes?
4. Three of the United States are nicknamed 'The Sunshine State'. Name two of them.
5. Who is welcome at a VVV in Holland?
6. St Lucia, Fort William, Malta, Dumbarton Castle, the Tower of London and the Cape of Good Hope were all proposed as being suitable for him. Who was he, and where did he go?

68

1. At the end of Wigan pier, a hump on the bank of the Leeds and Liverpool canal, from where coal was put into barges.
2. The Andaman and Nicobar Islands.
3. The coracle.
4. Churned curd – fresh, natural yoghurt.
5. The East River, New York.
6. The Hong Kong and Shanghai Bank.

143

1. Andy Warhol, in 1975.
2. Rwanda.
3. On the River Thames.
4. It is one of the exhibits in the Gandhi Museum, near his ashram.
5. Nevis Island.
6. After Hore-Belisha, the Transport Minister who introduced them to London.

218

1. Cricket.
2. At Pagan, one of the three principal cities.
3. The Lake District.
4. Florida, New Mexico and South Dakota.
5. Any engaging tourist. It is the sign of the local tourist office.
6. Napoleon. To St Helena.

69

1. What did Flanders and Swann find 'a transport of delight'?
2. Which country is known as the 'Switzerland of South America', because it is a republic without access to the sea?
3. Which Leicestershire town is famous for its pork pies?
4. What is noteworthy about the newspaper *Osservatore Romano*?
5. The World Wildlife Fund was founded in 1961 by a small group concerned about the plight of wildlife in which part of the world?
6. Which international airport serves Berlin?

144

1. From which station did Paul Theroux set out on the journey which filled *The Great Railway Bazaar*?
2. Which country, to which the Spice Islands sought by Columbus belong, became independent in 1949?
3. Which was England's tallest cathedral?
4. In which part of Germany do the locals wear *Lederhosen*?
5. Where did Charlemagne establish his court, his 'new Rome', of which only the Palace Chapel still stands?
6. Which travellers dressed in a livery known as 'blood and custard'?

219

1. To whom did the *Eight Feet in the Andes* belong?
2. Sailing from Northern Tasmania to Melbourne, Victoria, which strait do you cross?
3. Where must Harris Tweed be spun, dyed and hand-woven by the islanders in their own homes to be legally marketed?
4. Ethiopia has been Christian since which century?
5. In which Belgian city is Van Eyck's *The Adoration of the Mystic Lamb* on display?
6. Which US route was nicknamed the 'underground railway'?

69

1. The London omnibus.
2. Bolivia.
3. Melton Mowbray.
4. It is published by the Vatican.
5. East Africa.
6. Schonefeld, in East Germany, and Tegel, in West Germany.

144

1. Waterloo.
2. Indonesia.
3. Old St Paul's, before the Fire.
4. Bavaria.
5. Aachen.
6. British Rail workers, just after nationalization.

219

1. Dervla Murphy, her daughter Rachel and Juana, the mule.
2. Bass Strait.
3. In the Outer Hebrides. It must also be made from pure Scottish wool.
4. The fourth century.
5. Bruges.
6. The route taken by slaves escaping from the South, before the Civil War.

70

1. What did Napoleon call 'the finest drawing room in Europe'?
2. Where did Plato teach philosophy in 398 BC?
3. Which English cathedral has two large circular windows, the Dean's Eye and the Bishop's Eye?
4. Aryavaidya, siddha and unani are three main types of what?
5. Where is Max Yasgur's farm?
6. Name the liner which at the time of her launch, in 1858, was five times the size of any ship afloat.

145

1. Which city's walls did Joshua blow down with his trumpet?
2. Sailing round the coast from Naples to Taranto which seas do you cross?
3. Wilkie Collins found the Cheesewring 'a sight which is worth a visit to Cornwall, even if Cornwall presented nothing else to see'. What is it?
4. What can you expect at a Kashmiri *wazwan*?
5. The water in this French town is always good, but it was once capital. Which town?
6. What was the maximum penalty for breaking the speed limit in Peking in the 1930s?

220

1. Why is Qurna, at the junction of the Tigris and Euphrates rivers in Iraq, of prime world significance?
2. Which planet was discovered by Herschel in 1781?
3. What did King Arthur receive at Dozmary Pool, on Bodmin Moor, according to tradition?
4. What meat is traditionally served at an Icelandic Christmas dinner?
5. Whose guest are you when you stay in a Spanish *parador*?
6. Which group of travellers inspired the hit record *Convoy*?

70

1. The Piazza San Marco in Venice.
2. In a grove called Academia, just outside Athens.
3. Lincoln.
4. Massage in India.
5. Woodstock, New York, site of the legendary festival.
6. The *Great Eastern*, designed by Brunel, who called it 'my great babe'.

145

1. Jericho's.
2. The Tyrrhenian and Ionian Seas.
3. Huge granite stones balanced on top of each other, the result of stratified erosion.
4. A feast. It is named after the *waza*, professional cooks who prepare it.
5. Vichy, capital of Occupied France in the Second World War.
6. Death.

220

1. Because it is the traditional site of the Garden of Eden.
2. Uranus.
3. His legendary sword, Excalibur.
4. Ptarmigan. The main festivities are held on Christmas Eve.
5. The Spanish government's. They are government-owned hotels, usually in historic buildings.
6. Truckers, who travel along the US highways in convoys.

71

1. Where is the Empty Quarter, into which Wilfred Thesiger travelled?
2. What structure in San Francisco was known as The Rock?
3. Which is the most easterly town in Britain?
4. The Eastern Orthodox Churches recognize four ancient patriarchates. Name two.
5. In which country is the garden of Ryoan-Ji?
6. The Duke of Wellington said, 'I see no reason to suppose that these machines will ever force themselves into general use.' Of which machines?

146

1. Which famous couple went to live at Valldemosa, in Majorca?
2. The father of the Kikuyu people was taken up a mountain by Mogai, the Creator, to see the land prepared for them. Which mountain?
3. What is unique about the mine at Winsford in Cheshire?
4. Where did the Tonton Macoute exercise a reign of terror?
5. When would you attend the German festival of *Fasching*?
6. What essential item of tackle did the Romans lack?

221

1. If reincarnated, how might Princess Anne spend a lot of time at the wheel?
2. In which country is Mount Kilimanjaro?
3. Where in Britain can you visit a replica of George Washington's garden at Mount Vernon, Virginia?
4. The Danes call them *wienerbrod*. What do we call them?
5. What was the name given to the slow passage through the Continent to Rome undertaken by wealthy young gentlemen?
6. Why are some of the Empire State Building's lights turned out at certain times of year?

71

1. The Arabian Desert. He wrote about his experiences in *Arabian Sands*.
2. Alcatraz, the prison.
3. Lowestoft.
4. Alexandria, Antioch, Jerusalem and Constantinople.
5. In Japan. The garden consists of rocks set into patterns of raked sand.
6. Of trains.

146

1. George Sand and Chopin. The house is now open to the public.
2. Mount Kenya.
3. It is the only rock salt mine in Britain.
4. In Haiti. They were Papa Doc's security forces.
5. Just before Lent. (Rather similar to Mardi Gras.)
6. Stirrups.

221

1. She once whimsically suggested that she might have been a long-distance trucker in another life.
2. Tanzania. It is Africa's highest mountain.
3. At Claverton Manor, the American Museum near Bath.
4. Danish pastries.
5. 'The Grand Tour', popular in the eighteenth century.
6. Because migratory birds become confused in their direction if the lights are left on.

72

1. Who found himself *Among the Russians*?
2. What links Alderney, Jersey and Guernsey with San Clemente, Anacapa and San Miguel?
3. The Bishop of London departed in 1975 after an unbroken run of 1,284 years. From where?
4. What happens at the annual Car Festival of the Jagganath Temple in Puri, India?
5. Name the place to which Monet retired to paint water-lilies.
6. When did 'wheeler-dealers' first start getting their palms greased?

147

1. During his travels King Edward VII put in to Gibraltar and 'passed two nights at the Convent'. Explain.
2. By what name are the Falkland Islands known in Argentina?
3. Which village met, and beat, All England at 'bat and ball'?
4. Why has no one ever climbed the Mountain of Pity in Mexico?
5. Near which city is Peterhof, Peter the Great's palace?
6. What did 'triremes' have three of?

222

1. Who was the real-life model for Robinson Crusoe?
2. In 1788 Captain Phillip, a British sailor, established a settlement at Port Jackson near Botany Bay. Later it was renamed after the British Home Secretary. What is it now?
3. What is the shortest distance by road between Land's End and John O'Groats?
4. What is the name given to people of French Canadian extraction, who live in the southern states of America?
5. A visit to South Africa's botanic gardens at Kirstenbosch is interesting because of its unique policy. Which?
6. What are *cargadores* on Mexico's railway stations?

72

1. Colin Thubron.
2. The former are part of the Channel Islands, the latter the Californian Channel Islands.
3. Fulham Palace.
4. Huge chariots, carrying statues, are dragged along by devotees of the god, from whose name the word 'juggernaut' is derived.
5. Giverny, some way south of Paris.
6. 1946 onwards. UK domestic car sales were restricted in favour of exports, thus boosting the second-hand market, and bringing a new phrase into the language to describe used-car dealers.

147

1. It is the name of the Government House there.
2. *Las Islas Malvinas*.
3. Hambledon, Hants., at the end of the eighteenth century.
4. Because it is the nickname of the National Pawn Shop in Mexico City.
5. Leningrad, once St Petersburg.
6. Banks of oars. Triremes were ancient warships.

222

1. Alexander Selkirk.
2. Sydney.
3. 877 miles. (Accept to within 25 miles either side.)
4. Cajun.
5. Only plants indigenous to South Africa are grown there.
6. Porters.

73

1. What aids to speedy travel did Hermes employ?
2. What is the name of the theory generally expounded by geographers to explain 'continental drift'?
3. Where would you go to see Ogham stones?
4. Name one of the two chief sects of the Pennsylvania Dutch.
5. Where is Britain's National Museum of Photography, Film and Television?
6. Which world airline has the largest fleet of aircraft?

148

1. The story of Count Dracula is based on the legend of Vlad the Impaler of Transylvania. Where is Transylvania?
2. What is the name of the port of Athens?
3. Which London landmark was hailed by the *Daily Herald* as 'a flaming altar of the modern temple of power'?
4. How many stripes are there on the US national flag?
5. Which controversial building resulted from a competition won by Richard Rogers and Renzo Piano in 1971?
6. What is the name of Kenya's main airport?

223

1. Which doughty woman traveller chose the little town of Asolo, in Italy, as her home?
2. Known to the Romans as Deva, and to the ancient Britons as Caerleon, how is this city known to us?
3. Where is the smallest cathedral in England?
4. Chapultepec Park provides a green space for the citizens of which highly polluted city?
5. Where would you go to see Lutyens' reconstruction of a Mogul garden?
6. In which country did the 'Lunatic Line' finally reach the Mountains of the Moon?

73

1. He wore winged sandals and sometimes added wings to his hat.
2. Plate tectonics.
3. Ireland. They are ancient Irish standing stones.
4. The Amish and the Mennonites. (They may also live in Ohio and Indiana.)
5. At Bradford.
6. Aeroflot.

148

1. In Romania.
2. Piraeus.
3. Battersea Power Station, when it was opened in 1933.
4. Thirteen. In 1818 Congress fixed on thirteen, the number of the original colonies.
5. The Beaubourg arts centre in Paris.
6. Jomo Kenyatta, named after Kenya's first president.

223

1. Freya Stark. Browning and Shelley also lived there for a time.
2. Chester.
3. Oxford.
4. Mexico City.
5. India – the gardens of the Rashtrapati Bhavan, the former viceroy's house, now home of the president.
6. In Uganda. The East African railway was mocked as the 'lunatic line', 'from nowhere, through nowhere, to nowhere', when construction started in 1898.

74

1. Which travellers to India in the early nineteenth century were known as 'the Fishing Fleet'?
2. Which is the only South American republic with both Atlantic and Pacific coastlines?
3. Name the island which has the highest sea-cliffs in Ireland, at 1,950 ft. above sea-level?
4. In which Spanish town are young bulls let loose in the streets on the feast-day of San Fermin?
5. Where is the Statue of Liberty, other than in New York?
6. Name one of the three ships which travelled with Columbus in search of the New World.

149

1. In which country were *King Solomon's Mines* situated?
2. Which is the only borough of New York city on the mainland?
3. What cargo was the Ffestiniog steam railway built to carry?
4. In which country is the birthday of Benito Juarez a national holiday?
5. A boat trip on which river would take you to Mandalay?
6. What traditionally provides the power for a Lapp's *pulkka*, a boat-shaped sledge?

224

1. Why did Blériot pick up a prize of £1,000 in 1900?
2. What do Abu Dhabi, Ajman, Dubai, Fujeirah, Rasal Khaimah, Sharjah and Umm al Qaiwain together make up?
3. Where can you ride on a tram, eat rock and look at the Illuminations?
4. Where does Amaretto, the almond liqueur, come from?
5. What could be wrong with going for gold in Acapulco?
6. Which Himalayan kingdom has no railways, no airstrips and no navigable rivers?

74

1. Young British women carried by the new P&O steamers, who came to catch a husband.
2. Colombia.
3. Achill Island.
4. In Pamplona.
5. In Paris. A smaller prototype stands by the River Seine.
6. The *Niña*, the *Pinta* and the *Santa Maria*.

149

1. In Israel.
2. The Bronx. Brooklyn and Queens are on Long Island, Manhattan on Manhattan Island, Richmond on Staten Island.
3. Slate. (Blaenau Ffestiniog was once the slate capital of Wales.)
4. In Mexico.
5. The Irrawaddy – like the River Kwai, it is in Burma.
6. The *pulkka* is harnessed to a reindeer.

224

1. He was the first pilot to fly the English Channel. The prize was awarded by the *Daily Mail*.
2. The United Arab Emirates.
3. In Blackpool.
4. Saronno, in Italy.
5. Acapulco gold is a name given to a type of marijuana.
6. Bhutan. People get around by bus.

75

1. What sort of vehicle is Dr Who's Tardis?
2. The Sahara Desert extends into ten countries. Name five.
3. Where are millions of pictures of Nottingham Castle to be found?
4. By 1980 figures, which people are reckoned to have the heaviest per capita rate of beer consumption?
5. Who said, 'There's not a place in the world I'd rather live than on the Monterey peninsula. I plan to stay for ever'?
6. Who was the first human in space, launched on 12 April 1961?

150

1. What was the home town of Doña Inés which was, according to Byron, 'famous for women and oranges'?
2. Who first wrote of an unknown southern land, known until the fifteenth century as Terra Australis Incognita?
3. Edward Burra always referred to it as Tinkerbell Town. What?
4. How can you tell Rhine wines from Mosel wines at a glance?
5. The gates of the Royal Botanic Gardens at Pamplemousses won a prize at the Crystal Palace Exhibition. Where are they?
6. What do you get if you cross Mikoyan and Gurevich?

225

1. Which city was Jonah trying to avoid when he was swallowed by a whale?
2. What was peculiar about Kitchener's plans to rebuild Khartoum?
3. Which two towns in the south-west were linked by the Roman road Ackling Dyke?
4. Which country switched from Arabic script to the Roman alphabet in 1928?
5. Which Fleet Street pub was frequented by Johnson, Boswell and Goldsmith, among others?
6. What does form E111 do for you if you take it abroad?

75

1. A time machine, looking like a London police box.
2. Algeria, Chad, Egypt (the United Arab Republic), Libya, Mali, Mauretania, Morocco, Niger, the Sudan and Tunisia.
3. On the backs of packets of Players' cigarettes.
4. The Germans – then the Czechs, with the Australians third.
5. Clint Eastwood.
6. Yuri Gagarin (in a Vostok spacecraft).

150

1. Seville.
2. Ptolemy, the second-century Greek philosopher.
3. Rye.
4. Rhine wines are bottled in brown bottles, Mosel wines in green.
5. On the island of Mauritius.
6. A MiG – the best-known line of Soviet fighter aircraft.

225

1. Nineveh.
2. He laid out the city in the shape of the Union Jack.
3. Dorchester and Salisbury.
4. Turkey.
5. The Cheshire Cheese.
6. It activates reciprocal free or reduced cost health care agreements between Britain and most European countries.

FOR THE BEST IN PAPERBACKS, LOOK FOR THE

In every corner of the world, on every subject under the sun, Penguin represents quality and variety – the very best in publishing today.

For complete information about books available from Penguin – including Pelicans, Puffins, Peregrines and Penguin Classics – and how to order them, write to us at the appropriate address below. Please note that for copyright reasons the selection of books varies from country to country.

In the United Kingdom: For a complete list of books available from Penguin in the U.K., please write to *Dept E.P., Penguin Books Ltd, Harmondsworth, Middlesex, UB7 0DA*

In the United States: For a complete list of books available from Penguin in the U.S., please write to *Dept BA, Penguin, 299 Murray Hill Parkway, East Rutherford, New Jersey 07073*

In Canada: For a complete list of books available from Penguin in Canada, please write to *Penguin Books Canada Ltd, 2801 John Street, Markham, Ontario L3R 1B4*

In Australia: For a complete list of books available from Penguin in Australia, please write to the *Marketing Department, Penguin Books Australia Ltd, P.O. Box 257, Ringwood, Victoria 3134*

In New Zealand: For a complete list of books available from Penguin in New Zealand, please write to the *Marketing Department, Penguin Books (NZ) Ltd, Private Bag, Takapuna, Auckland 9*

In India: For a complete list of books available from Penguin, please write to *Penguin Overseas Ltd, 706 Eros Apartments, 56 Nehru Place, New Delhi, 110019*

In Holland: For a complete list of books available from Penguin in Holland, please write to *Penguin Books Nederland B.V., Postbus 195, NL–1380AD Weesp, Netherlands*

In Germany: For a complete list of books available from Penguin, please write to *Penguin Books Ltd, Friedrichstrasse 10 – 12, D–6000 Frankfurt Main 1, Federal Republic of Germany*

In Spain: For a complete list of books available from Penguin in Spain, please write to *Longman Penguin España, Calle San Nicolas 15, E–28013 Madrid, Spain*

A CHOICE OF PENGUINS

The Book Quiz Book   Joseph Connolly

Who was literature's performing flea . . .? Who wrote 'Live Now, Pay Later . . .'? Keats and Cartland, Balzac and Braine, Coleridge conundrums, Eliot enigmas, Tolstoy teasers . . . all in this brilliant quiz book. You will be on the shelf without it . . .

Voyage through the Antarctic   Richard Adams and Ronald Lockley

Here is the true, authentic Antarctic of today, brought vividly to life by Richard Adams, author of *Watership Down*, and Ronald Lockley, the world-famous naturalist. 'A good adventure story, with a lot of information and a deal of enthusiasm for Antarctica and its animals' – *Nature*

Getting to Know the General   Graham Greene

'In August 1981 my bag was packed for my fifth visit to Panama when the news came to me over the telephone of the death of General Omar Torrijos Herrera, my friend and host . . .' 'Vigorous, deeply felt, at times funny, and for Greene surprisingly frank' – *Sunday Times*

Television Today and Tomorrow: Wall to Wall Dallas?
Christopher Dunkley

Virtually every British home has a television, nearly half now have two sets or more, and we are promised that before the end of the century there will be a vast expansion of television delivered via cable and satellite. How did television come to be so central to our lives? Is British television really the best in the world, as politicians like to assert?

Arabian Sands   Wilfred Thesiger

'In the tradition of Burton, Doughty, Lawrence, Philby and Thomas, it is, very likely, the book about Arabia to end all books about Arabia' – *Daily Telegraph*

When the Wind Blows   Raymond Briggs

'A visual parable against nuclear war: all the more chilling for being in the form of a strip cartoon' – *Sunday Times*. 'The most eloquent anti-Bomb statement you are likely to read' – *Daily Mail*

A CHOICE OF PENGUINS

A Fortunate Grandchild 'Miss Read'

Grandma Read in Lewisham and Grandma Shafe in Walton on the Naze were totally different in appearance and outlook, but united in their affection for their grand-daughter – who grew up to become the much-loved and popular novelist.

The Ultimate Trivia Quiz Game Book Maureen and Alan Hiron

If you are immersed in trivia, addicted to quiz games, endlessly nosey, then this is the book for you. Over 10,000 pieces of utterly dispensable information!

The Diary of Virginia Woolf
Five volumes, edited by Quentin Bell and Anne Olivier Bell

'As an account of the intellectual and cultural life of our century, Virginia Woolf's diaries are invaluable; as the record of one bruised and unquiet mind, they are unique'– Peter Ackroyd in the *Sunday Times*

Voices of the Old Sea Norman Lewis

'I will wager that *Voices of the Old Sea* will be a classic in the literature about Spain' – *Mail on Sunday*. 'Limpidly and lovingly Norman Lewis has caught the helpless, unwitting, often foolish, but always hopeful village in its dying summers, and saved the tragedy with sublime comedy' – *Observer*

The First World War A. J. P. Taylor

In this superb illustrated history, A. J. P. Taylor 'manages to say almost everything that is important for an understanding and, indeed, intellectual digestion of that vast event . . . A special text . . . a remarkable collection of photographs' – *Observer*

Ninety-Two Days Evelyn Waugh

With characteristic honesty, Evelyn Waugh here debunks the romantic notions attached to rough travelling: his journey in Guiana and Brazil is difficult, dangerous and extremely uncomfortable, and his account of it is witty and unquestionably compelling.

FOR THE BEST IN PAPERBACKS, LOOK FOR THE

PENGUIN OMNIBUSES

More Stories from Thrush Green 'Miss Read'

Gossip, squabbles, domestic drama and the quiet rhythms of country living – this is the world of 'Miss Read'. And here, in one volume, is some of the best of that world: *Battles at Thrush Green*, *Return to Thrush Green* and *Gossip from Thrush Green*.

The Alexander Trilogy Mary Renault

'One of this century's most original works of art' – Gore Vidal. Mary Renault's masterly evocation of ancient Greece and of Alexander the Great, published in one volume: *Fire From Heaven*, *The Persian Boy* and *Funeral Games*.

The Collected Stories of Eudora Welty

'The publication of these *Collected Stories* allows us to celebrate the achievement of one of the most entertaining, evocative – and underrated – of American writers' – *The Times Literary Supplement*

The First Rumpole Omnibus John Mortimer

'A fruity, foxy masterpiece, defender of our wilting faith in mankind' – *Sunday Times*. Here is Horace Rumpole, triumphantly celebrated in this first omnibus edition: *Rumpole of the Bailey*, *The Trials of Rumpole* and *Rumpole's Return*.

The Best of Roald Dahl

Twenty tales to curdle your blood and scorch your soul, chosen from his bestsellers *Over to You*, *Someone Like You*, *Kiss Kiss* and *Switch Bitch*.

The Collected Stories of Elizabeth Bowen
with an Introduction by Angus Wilson

'She is a major writer . . . the link that connects Virginia Woolf with Iris Murdoch and Muriel Spark' – Victoria Glendinning. A selection of seventy-nine stories – love stories, ghost stories, stories of childhood, of English middle-class life in the twenties and thirties, of London during the Blitz – that show the varied skills of a master writer at her best.